The Powerful Book of Protection Spells

A Witch's Guide to Defending Against Negative Energy, Psychic Attacks, Curses, and Harmful Spirits

Layla Moon

Layla Moon

Table of Contents

4 FREE Gifts

To help you along your spiritual journey, I've created 4 FREE bonus eBooks.

You can get instant access by signing up to my email newsletter below.

On top of the 4 free books, you will also receive weekly tips along with free book giveaways, discounts, and so much more.

All of these bonuses are 100% free with no strings attached. You don't need to provide any personal information except your email address.

To get your bonus, go to:

https://dreamlifepress.com/four-free-gifts

Or scan the QR code below

SCAN ME

Spirit Guides for Beginners: How to Hear the Universe's Call and Communicate with Your Spirit Guide and Guardian Angels

Guided by Moon herself, inspired by her own experiences and knowledge that has been passed down by hundreds of generations for thousands of years, you'll discover everything you need to know to;

- Understanding what the call of the universe is
- How to hear and comprehend it
- Knowing who and what your spirit guides and guardian angels are
- Learning how to connect, start a conversation, and listen to your guides
- How to manifest your dreams with the help of the cosmic source
- Learning how to start living the life you want to live
- And so much more…

Law of Attraction: Manifest Your Desire

Learn how to tap into the infinite power of the universe and manifest everything you want in life.

Includes:

- Law of Attraction: Manifest Your Desire ebook
- Law of Attraction Workbook
- Cheat sheets and checklists so make sure you're on the right path

Hoodoo Book of Spells for Beginners: Easy and effective Rootwork, Conjuring, and Protection Spells for Healing and Prosperity

Harness the power of one of the greatest magics. Hoodoo is a powerful force ideal for holding negativity at bay, promoting positivity in all areas in your life, offering protection to the things you love, and ultimately taking control of your destiny.

Inside, you will discover:

- How to get started with Hoodoo in your day-to-day life
- How to use conjuration spells to manifest the life you want to live
- How casting protection spells can help you withstand the toughest of times
- Break cycles of bad luck and promote good fortune throughout your life
- Hoodoo to encourage prosperity and financial stability
- How to heal using Hoodoo magic, both short-term and long-term traumas and troubles
- Remove curses and banish pain, suffering, and negativity from your life
- And so much more...

Book of Shadows

A printable PDF to support you in your spiritual transformation.

Within the pages, you will find:
- Potion and tinctures tracking sheet
- Essential oils log pages
- Herbs log pages
- Magical rituals and spiritual body goals checklist
- Tarot reading spread sheets
- Weekly moon and planetary cycle tracker
- And so much more

Get all the resources for FREE by visiting the link below

https://dreamlifepress.com/four-free-gifts

Introduction

Hoping for the best, prepared for the worst, and unsurprised by anything in between.
–Maya Angelou

Everyone needs to feel safe, even the strongest person you know. What do you do when the standard protection practices aren't enough? Some folks just make do with what they have and hope for the best. They don't realize that they hold the power to change their circumstances. Although things happen that are out of their control, that doesn't mean they have to hand over full dominance to fate.

Others, like me, turn to witchcraft. Spellwork has been my savior. I'm in my thirties now and have turned my life around from constantly worrying about how I'm going to take care of myself and my baby to actually having a purpose in life. Like all humans, I still struggle, but now I have the tools to deal with situations as they come at me.

I have found that protection spells are the best defense against all sorts of situations like physical attack, psychic attack, financial trouble, vehicle issues, and anything else Murphy's Law can destroy.

I'm not going to claim that spells can shield you from every single problem in your life. We're human, after all. If we could wave a hand and say a few words to skirt around every obstacle in our paths, everyone would be a witch. Everyone would also be bored to tears for lack of challenges. Challenge is how we evolve on this planet. What spellwork *can* do is twist the odds in your favor, increasing your chances for success—maybe even survival.

One night, I had to take the bus home from work. My car had broken down and I didn't have cab fare. I do a short protection spell every day before work, but I was still nervous. There was a creepy man staring at me from the back of the bus. I could feel his slimy gaze drilling into the back of my head. I looked back a couple of times and he didn't even bother to avert his eyes. He just blatantly ogled me until I faced forward again.

The bus stopped and I hurried off, anxious to get home. My heart raced as he got off behind me. I sped up and he kept pace a few feet behind me. I was so scared I wanted to cry. Instead, I tried to ignore him and kept walking toward my building. I pictured a barrier around me and chanted, "Goddess, protect me," under my breath repeatedly. After a couple more steps, the

creep suddenly turned around and headed in the opposite direction.

Was it the spell, or is that the way life works sometimes? It could be either, but I'm certain it was the spell for one reason. Once a predator has you in their sight, they will not stop unless they no longer see you as easy prey. Nobody else was on that street. I was as alone as ever but he changed his mind. That is witchcraft. I turned the odds in my favor and against him. Everybody ends up in sticky situations but with a witchy edge, they will be easier to manage.

Protection spells aren't just for dangerous situations. You can do a spell to protect your energy field when you have to speak in front of a crowd, make that nagging coworker leave you alone for once, or protect your car from getting dinged in the parking lot. All these types of protection spells could each fill up a book on their own. You need to know the possibilities, but I am going to teach you witchcraft specific spellwork. You'll learn spells to ward against psychic attack, bad energy, curses, and spirits. Every witch should know these types of spells. They are important to your craft and your wellbeing. The world of unseen forces comes with unseen dangers that every witch should be aware of.

But why?

"Those who don't practice witchcraft don't experience these things, so you must be attracting them."

I have heard that so many times through the years. It's true in the sense that when you start, your energy field changes, and energetic beings will be curious. Most of the time this is harmless. The statement is also misleading. These things do happen to normal folks. Their luck turns sour for no reason, they're unexplainably moody when a certain person enters a room only to have it disappear when they leave, or they have a sudden onset of sleep paralysis with no cause.

People with no magickal experience don't know why these things happen and can't do anything about them, so they blow it off and forget. Witches have no such luxury. We know what's really going on underneath the surface and have the skills to do something about it.

Notice I said, "skills," and not, "power." Anyone can learn witchcraft if they're willing to put in the time and practice. Some will be more talented than others, like with any other job, but it can be learned. You don't have to be born with certain abilities, and you don't have to have witches in your bloodline. You also don't have to be initiated into some secret society by a weird smelling naked guy to practice magick. Initiates practice their form of magick, which is kept secret to outsiders, but you are free to practice your own form of magick without permission of any other being. You do you, and pay no attention to the naysayers. Chances are, they're on a power trip and determined to keep everyone else under their bootheels.

What I'm going to show you is a collection of spells that are easy enough for a beginner and potent enough to get the job done. You won't need a bunch of fancy tools or hard-to-find ingredients. You *will* need a healthy imagination and a real desire to accomplish your goals. Imagination is the center of creation. That is one of this witch's secrets. When people say "visualize," they should be saying "imagine." I'm guilty of this myself. It's not enough to see your goal like you're watching TV. All your senses have to be active for the spell to manifest your goal.

If you charge a necklace to place a protective barrier around you when you wear it, what will that barrier look like? How will it come out of the necklace to surround you? Will it make a noise? Does it have a certain smell (like an herb you used in the spell), or texture? What color is it? This may seem complicated, but it happens in a split second after you've practiced for a while. This imagination is the key ingredient in any type of spell you choose to do. I wonder if whoever came up with, "It's just your imagination," knew this and wanted to keep it to themselves.

Witchcraft is a way of life and for some, a religion. It requires study, hard work, and endless self-examination. Witchy thinking doesn't only include spells and silly rhymes—you learn to meditate, discern and work with different energies, get to know other realities and their inhabitants, and learn to understand what you really need in life. Many people know what they *want*, but few know what they *need*. Learn to slow down and feed your soul. Don't get sucked into the addiction of instant gratification.

Most witches you will find in the community are also science enthusiasts. This happened organically, but it's a very good thing. If you don't balance magick and science, then you don't balance your inner and outer worlds. On the inside, you can be the most powerful witch in the world, but on the outside, you may well be in a mental health facility for delusions. Another good side to this balance is that spellwork is like experimentation. We do spells because we want results. If the results aren't there, that spell is either reformed or discarded. Spiritual beliefs and different techniques can be added as the individual sees fit, but the energy behind the spell is the same. Every religion in every culture throughout time has had its own system of magick. It is my humble opinion that we all tap into the same power source in different ways.

Let's Get Salty

Salt is one of the main ingredients you'll come across when reading up on witchcraft. Table salt will do if you don't have any other kind. It's a powerful cleanser and protector and it's found in any grocery or convenience store. If you have nothing else, you should always have salt.

Salt should be used sparingly. You don't need a thick ring of it around you or the object you're protecting to do the job. A little goes a long way.

Please don't throw your salt or items containing it on the ground. It ruins the soil. If it's water, the toilet or sink will do. If it's solid, just throw it in the garbage. If you want to create a powder barrier around the outside of your home, powdered eggshell is a wonderful substitute.

Now it's time for the spells! This book should be considered part of your self-defense arsenal along with your deadbolt and doorbell camera (or gun and pepper spray if that's your thing).

CHAPTER 1

Who am I?

If you know who you are then your ego feels safe instead of fearful, and is more open to exploration.

-Julia Woodman

So who am I and why should you listen to me? There are megatons of spell books out there and a lot of those focus on protection. Different people have different experiences, and I may have something to offer that you haven't read before.

I grew up in Brooklyn, New York. As you can imagine, a young woman of color in the city has her own set of challenges on top of the normal human condition—gang violence, muggings, others claiming your body as theirs, and being invisible otherwise. I got pregnant in high school. My parents were a big help with the baby, and I took a night job so I could provide for us and get my diploma. We moved out on our own right after graduation. My folks and I fought too much about my lifestyle choices and parenting style.

I can't lie. I thought it would be easy. I was a dumb kid who assumed that I could just find a neighbor to look after the baby while I worked a single job—in New York City. Reality quickly slapped me upside the head as I struggled to find more work. Kids are expensive.

Although I didn't realize it at the time, I desperately wanted to find someone to love me that didn't need a diaper change. I craved adult connection, so I dated. A lot. I was at least smart enough to kick them to the curb when they showed their true personalities. I was 24 when I finally gave up. I decided that finding a good man was impossible. Maybe it was a dream, and all men were toxic. After a bout of severe depression, I realized that my little man was the only important one in my life. I made a pact to only focus on his wellbeing and do my best to raise him right.

Toddler in tow, I decided to go to the bookstore just to get out of the house. I stumbled upon a book called *The Law of Attraction: The Basics of the Teachings of Abraham* by Esther and Jerry Hicks. Something clicked when I read the blurb. The thought that I could manifest a better life for my child and I was mind blowing. I was also skeptical. I circled the store one more time, glancing at titles but my mind was still on that book. I grabbed it when we came full circle and I spent my meager lunch budget on it.

I didn't regret my growling stomach that week. What I learned more than made up for the missed meals. Not only did I find the power to manifest my best life, but also gained the mental clarity to gear myself up for success. It's not enough to do spellwork, you have to believe you deserve it.

I read every book I could get my hands on that could bring positive change into my life. I have since incorporated witchcraft and hoodoo into my practice and life keeps getting better and better for me and my boy.

The first thing I manifested was a better job with in-house daycare. The most important thing to me was the ability to be there for my son when he needed me. I then worked to pay off all my debts and eventually move to a better apartment. I got an online degree that landed me a raise. I was still lonely, but I was just too busy to notice. By then, I was solely focused on protection magick. I needed to protect my new standing in life, my child, and myself as I survived life in the city.

Along the way I made some great friends in the magickal community, which helped alleviate the loneliness. Three years ago, I met someone online. I know, it's counter intuitive to the idea of protection. I did a background check on him and then read tarot on whether I should meet him for coffee. The check didn't show anything remarkable. He was divorced with two kids who lived with their mother, had a decent job, and lived in a lower middle class neighborhood. He worked hard and didn't spend all his free time partying. The reading came out well. The cards even indicated that he would get a promotion soon. So I took the risk and met him for coffee.

He is the best boyfriend I could ever hope for. He is mild-mannered, great with my son, and he's shown interest in witchcraft. We rarely fight and always have fun when we get together. We both want to keep our own spaces and neither of us want more kids. That may change in the future, but we're not rushing. I didn't do a spell to find him. When you practice magick for a while, things will line up on their own. You're actively working to raise your energy level to suit your highest good and the universe sees that.

Common Ingredients for Spells

There are many tools, curios, and botanicals to cast your spells with. Witchcraft is a huge market nowadays. I began like many. I wanted to buy everything that every book said I needed. I was drawn in by those beautiful toys and home decor items. I wanted everything that proclaimed me as a witch. I bought what little I could, but all my spare money was for my son. When I read my first book on hoodoo, it clicked. Hoodoo emphasizes using what you have available and putting enough power behind it to get great results. Feel free to use all the pretty things if you like, but I personally get better results when I use what I have or can pick up at the grocery store. This is not a book on hoodoo. It's a combination of everything I've learned over the years with the "go with what you got" outlook. Step out of the materialism trap and focus only on what you need.

Dollar stores are fantastic witchy markets, too. Besides salt, here are a few ingredients you can get on your way home from work.

- Pepper is great for banishing and protection. Black pepper and red pepper flakes are my favorites.

- Rosemary is perfect for cleansing your aura. I like to steep it and put it into a spray bottle. You can drink it as a tea to cleanse your energy, inside and out.

- Coffee speeds up the process of any spell.

- Star anise opens up your psychic awareness and helps you determine what you need protection from.

- Candles can be the emergency or glass ones from the dollar store. On many occasions, I've made do with air freshener candles and they've worked great. Tealights are inexpensive and come in big packages. Their burn time is usually perfect for most spells.

- Incense from these stores aren't the best quality, but they will do in a pinch. Make sure the area is well ventilated when burning them, though.

- A collection of sharp objects (be careful!) are great to put in spell bottles and charm bags. Broken glass, pins, needles, and nails are the easiest to get.

- Pen and paper are essential to any witchcraft practice. You will write out petitions and name papers, create your sigils, and make your own intention statements.

- If music is your thing, a music player comes in handy to get you in the mood.

- A long lighter for your candles and paper is important, especially if you like the seven day glass candles.

- You should have a metal or otherwise fireproof bowl for burning petitions and sigils—or whatever else needs burning.

- If you're going to burn things, make sure to have a fire extinguisher handy. Never leave candles or anything else burning. Make sure everything is out and cool to the touch when you're done.

Now you have a basic supply list that you can build on as time goes by—and don't forget, nature can provide everything you need. Anything that corresponds to the elements of earth, air, fire, water, and spirit will accomplish every goal you have.

Protection is Important

Someone once asked me, "Why do you need protection spells? We have guns."

This person obviously had no clue about the spiritual world. I have encountered dangerous spirits, astral parasites (these are mindless beings that like to latch onto your aura), evil practitioners that curse people for no reason, and new practitioners that haven't learned to properly close the magickal gateways they've opened.

There are also the haters you meet in your daily life. They don't know they're casting magick at you, but their bad feelings cling and cause anything from sudden lethargy to a run of bad luck. This is the Evil Eye—a curse born of envy. These also include energy vampires. They usually don't know they're doing it, but they drain the energy right out of you. You'll feel depressed and tired after dealing with them. They'll feel better when they leave you, but soon they're back with more of the same. They become junkies for your power because they can't maintain their own. There's no need to attack these people. Just protect your aura and you'll be fine. Everyone has experienced these things from time to time, even if they weren't aware of it. Being aware is preferrable. Ignorance is not bliss, trust me.

Demonic possession is not as common as the media would have you believe, at least in the biblical sense. There are those who use ritual possession as part of their religion, but that is vastly different from what I'm talking about. I have only seen one case of fire-and-brimstone possession. I made up an exorcism ritual on the spot and it worked, but not before the puking and speaking in tongues. The sad thing is, the demon made the possessed person feel powerful. A couple of weeks later they asked for it to come back. I never saw this person again. That was enough to make me realize that it does happen, even if rarely, and to be ready for it.

Earthly spirits such as ghosts and land spirits are the most curious beings I've ever come across. When I cast a circle or light a candle, there is always a spirit that pops up to be nosy. They have serious boundary issues. Don't be afraid to tell them to mind their business and throw some salt at them if they don't listen the first time. Usually, they'll amble away once they see what's happening. If they are too stubborn and are bothering you, do a full cleansing and make it known that they aren't welcome.

Everyday people are your biggest enemy. They come with their own psychic baggage and that tends to cling to the people around them. They don't realize it and neither do the people they encounter. As you start to develop your psychic senses, you'll be able to tell when this happens and take care of it as it comes. One of the most important lessons I've learned is that there is a reason that some people attract toxic people in their lives and others attract decent human beings. The energy of the last person you were with will stick, attracting more of the same. It often leads to a cycle of negativity that is almost impossible to break. I will teach you how to clean off the lingering vibes and put up a barrier to keep it from happening again.

One more danger that I've rarely seen mentioned is the company you keep, including where you work. The longer you're in close contact with someone, the more your energies start to sync up. This has been especially detrimental to my friends who work in the medical field. I've known people who have worked in nursing homes, hospitals, and with the developmentally challenged. Caring for others is draining, but more so for people in these fields. Not only do you have to deal with your own empathy for those in your care, but you also have to guard yourself so your energy doesn't match theirs. A way to tell if this is starting to happen is to watch your mannerisms and figures of speech. Perhaps a patient says something you find cute or funny, so you start saying it. You'll start to mimic each other's gestures and facial expressions. Soon, you'll start to mentally feel like the patient. If they're depressed, so are you. If they have memory problems or behavioral issues, so will you. You must be vigilant with your cleansing and protection in the world of healthcare.

Cultural Appropriation

I am an eclectic witch. I have studied and practiced many types of magick from many cultures. I will not claim to be a member of any of these cultures—I'm a millennial from Brooklyn. I believe in being well informed so I can find the right type of spell for a situation. Every culture has a nugget of truth, just like every mythology has a flood story. Granted, there are closed religious systems specific to certain cultures that I won't touch. Witchcraft is the practice of magick, not a religious system that incorporates it. I do pray to the Goddess occasionally, as I see the earth as the Great Goddess. She gave birth to us all and sustains us even when we abuse her.

I will not ask anyone else to believe the same thing, but I will ask you to believe that you can take back some control over your own life through spellwork. Stop running through other people's mazes and carve out your own. Believe in yourself and magick will happen. After all, the greatest thing about being human is free will.

Takeaway

In this chapter, you've learned:

- Who I am and how my practice could help you.

- Which basic ingredients you should have on hand.

- Why protection is important.

- My disclaimer on cultural appropriation.

CHAPTER 2

Casting the Spell

Energy can Neither be Created nor Destroyed.
–Albert Einstein

What is spellcasting?

Not everyone who picks up this book will be an experienced witch, so here are some basics you should know. Feel free to skip ahead if you know what you're doing.

Casting a spell is combining desire, imagination, and corresponding ingredients to cause a change in real life. These components together move the energy to work on your goal. If you are part of a certain tradition, calling on your deities and other powers will lend more energy toward that goal. If you don't follow a tradition and decide to do the work without the aid of deities or spirits, that's fine. You can work with what energy you've got handy.

By "energy," I don't mean the juice that you pay the electric bill for. It's the invisible force that gels this life together. Like a giant spider web, it connects everyone and everything. It goes into the past, present, and future. There are those of us who know how to navigate this web to bring us things we want and to banish things we don't want. We are inside it, trying to maneuver our way through. Spellcasting can make it easier, as we pluck pieces of the web and send it to do our bidding. There are countless ways of doing this, which is why I think every magick system has its merits.

Preparing to Cast Your Spell

First, you need to cleanse yourself. A bath, an herbal spray, or incense cleansing will get it done. This not only cleanses your aura of any lingering negativity, but serves to get you into the right frame of mind. You need to be calm and ready to cast. If you're still mad about that coworker gossiping about you, you need to be rid of that before doing a spell to protect your grandma.

If you know any divination techniques, you should use them. Ask if you're doing the right spell for the situation, if there's anything else you should work on top of protection, and in the case of casting for someone else, make sure you have the whole story.

Someone I know came to me crying that his ex-wife was trying to take their kids away. He asked me to do a protection for him and the two boys and a banishing on his ex-wife. I don't work for money but when I feel the cause is just, I will help. I did tarot readings before attempting any spellwork. In fact, I whipped out my cards right in front of him. I found out that he was only pretending to be the victim. He was actually an abusive drunk who hurt all three of them. I confronted him and he confessed. I learned that day just how important divination before spellwork is.

Now, you should decide what your goal is and the best spell to cast for it. Gather all the tools and ingredients, if any, you need. Don't forget the little things you may need, like a lighter if you're working with fire magick. Get everything set up so it's ready when you are. If you have to stop to look for something mid-spell, it could break your concentration. It won't nullify the spell or make it go crazy, it's just annoying and you'll have to get back into witch mode afterward.

Next, you have to get into the right frame of mind. It's time to shut out the real world and go into magick mode. There are tons of ways to get this done. Some meditate, some chant. I like to light a candle and incense, put on some music that matches the goal and get lost in it for a couple of songs. If I'm feeling extra blah, I'll put on music that makes me feel powerful. In time, you'll find a method that works best for you. The point is to forget about your ordinary life for a while.

If your music is on your phone, turn off all notifications. You don't want the distraction of your ringtone to ruin the mood. Also, make sure you won't be disturbed by anyone else in the house. Use earphones or earplugs if your place is noisy. It really does help you focus if you can stand having something in your ears the whole time.

Know When a Spell is Necessary

How do you know when you need a protection spell, especially if you've kept up with your daily protections? There are signs that will let you know, and divination will give you confirmation. Most of these signs have mundane causes as well, so rule those out first. If you feel sick, please see a doctor before jumping to conclusions.

- Sudden onset of headaches, nausea, and nosebleeds could indicate serious medical conditions. If a doctor has ruled them out, they could also be the result of an active psychic attack. By active, I mean the culprit knows exactly what they are doing and want you to suffer.

- Feeling drained when you go out in public means that your aura is overwhelmed by everyone around you. Energies clash and you get overstimulated. This is common and a basic barrier should take care of it.

- Sudden mood swings could be because of various medical issues, from mental illness to hormonal imbalance. If it's not those, then it's usually a sign of a spirit attachment, usually a ghost that's trying to get your attention. If that is accompanied by too many electrical and mechanical malfunctions to be a coincidence, then it could be demonic and you should immediately do a cleansing first, then protection.

- If you have pets, they can see things you can't. I've had both dogs and cats warn me of passing spirits in the house. They would stare off into space and sometimes growl at nothing. A friend had an African Grey parrot who would cry out, "Little boy! Come here!" The bird couldn't talk in full sentences, but I found out that the boy's name was Nathaniel and he liked to play doctor on the bird's missing toe.

- Other animals have been known to give warning, too. I've had an owl hoot at me every night until I did extra protections around myself and my son. I never heard from it again after that.

- Pay attention to your dreams. Unusual nightmares are generally a sign that you are under some kind of attack. I'm not talking about regular, naked in the classroom nightmares. These tend to get violent and leave you feeling ill the next day. Some are prone to night terrors, so this wouldn't apply to them.

Staying protected as a witch means noticing things that most would never think to look for and being competent enough to get rid of them. If in doubt, do a reading or have one done for you.

Other Ingredients You'll Need

I've already given the basic ingredients for protection spells. Those you should keep handy for any type of protection you need. Now, I want to give you a list of ingredients that you'll need just for this spellbook so you can have everything before you begin.

- a small mirror to hold a candle.

- Florida Water.

- selenite (optional).

- clear quartz (optional).

- bowls and utensils for mixing herbs.

- a fireproof bowl or something equally suitable for burning papers and herbs.

- organza bags.

- spray bottles.

- canisters and bottles with lids.

- a small plastic container with a locking lid.

- small dishes for your water and salt.

- a small gargoyle statue.

- a lighter to dedicate to the flamethrower spell.

- a charm for your vehicle.

- a red candle.

- lip balm.

- ammonia.

- lavender.

- a singing bowl or tambourine.

- a knife for symbolic cutting.

- string.

- poppy seeds.

- plain white rice.

- food coloring.

- spring water.

- nails.

- iron supplement pills as symbolic replacement for iron shavings.

- garlic.

- onions.

- ground cinnamon.

- ground cloves.

Timing

You've probably read a book or two that talks about how important it is to time your spell just right. You will notice that this book doesn't include instructions on timing. The simple reason is you can do protection work anytime you need it.

It does get a little more complicated though, as you delve deeper into the practice. Like colors and herbs, moon phases and astrology are boosters for your spellwork. They lend energy to make it a little more powerful, but aren't required for the magick to work. You are the spellcaster. If you think you need the extra power, there are several ways to get around the timing.

Charged Water

- You will need small sealable bottles and distilled water. Larger bottles are fine if you plan on using this method a lot. Distilled water doesn't spoil like tap water. You won't be drinking these.

- For a certain phase of the moon, set a bottle out when the sun goes down. Bring it in before bed (or before the sun comes up).

- For other astrological correspondences, set your bottles of water out during those times.

- For planetary waters, invoke the power of that planet into the water through imagination.

- Make sure to label your bottles. If any of them get cloudy or seem stale, replace them.

- Use them instead of other waters in your spells for that extra boost.

Astrological Candles

Each planet has its own color association, as does each zodiac sign. They also all have symbols that are easy to carve into a candle.

- Grab a candle of the color you need and carve the

appropriate symbol into it. Pillars are great for this because they can be used for similar spells later.

- You can also choose a candle that's appropriate for the spell and carve the symbol into it. This method is spell specific, so a smaller candle is advisable.

- You can have a personal power candle to light for every spell you do. This is a giant pillar candle of the appropriate color with your zodiac sign, name, and birthday carved into it.

Herbs

Herbs have astrological influences as well. Most of the herbs that you use will have the correct planet association for your spell already, so you don't have to do much. You can also choose to reinforce the association in your chants.

Working Backwards

If you want to work with magickal timing but need a spell right now, you can work backward to tailor the spell to the timing and the ingredients you have on hand.

Your paycheck was short, and you have one more bill to pay. On top of that, you have almost no food in the house. You need cash fast or your water will get turned off and you starve until next payday. The moon is waning, which is for banishing, so what can you do?

- Check your cupboard and the stash of fast food condiments you save (we all do it). You probably have some black pepper in there somewhere.

- Grab your bill (or a written representation of it if it's online) and cover it with the pepper.

- Hold your hands over the paper and imagine black light flowing into it. Say, "I banish this bill with all my might. This bill is gone as of tonight!"

- Leave it there. If it doesn't work, keep trying.

Instead of bringing money, you've banished your bill. That could bring you the money you need, but you may also get a notice that you were overcharged. That has happened to me twice.

Ok, you've done something about the bill, now what about the food? You desperately need groceries, and your stomach is growling hard.

- Place your hands on your stomach and close your eyes. Say, "Go away hunger, you'll eat soon."

- Give your tummy a reassuring pat.

You've just done a simple banishing of your hunger. That

doesn't mean you'll suddenly feel full, but it could mean someone will call you up and invite you out, or a neighbor will give you a box of dry goods they don't need. Maybe you will find a five dollar bill on the ground that will buy you beans and rice to tide you over until payday.

You should be proactive during this time. Check food banks, ask if the water company will let you pay in installments, and research assistance programs in your area. A spell will bring your goal closer, but most of the time it won't drop it into your lap. If you don't take an active role in your spells, the universe may decide that you don't really need them.

Why the Rhyme?

You'll notice that most of my spells have short and sweet rhymes. This serves several purposes. It tells both your subconscious and the universe what to do, and it's easier to write and memorize. Feel free to customize these however you want. My goal is to give you simple yet powerful spells that can be used any time. This is my method of spellcasting and it works for me. I hope it works for you, too.

Not all the spells rhyme, though. You'll notice that some are just short statements of intent. They're still easy to remember and are just there to vocalize what you're imagining. You don't have to say any of them out loud. The words combined with the pictures in your mind help direct the spell where it needs to go.

You've seen a movie or show where the person casting the spell recites a dark incantation in some dead language, right? They have to get the pronunciation just right or the spell won't work. Actually, the opposite is true. Unless you know exactly what you are saying, someone else's language won't help you. The spell you're doing is about your own knowledge and power, so use what you know. I've accomplished more with, "Get off me!" than with any ritual to banish ghosts that lasts for hours and leaves me exhausted. If it makes sense to you, it will make sense to the universe.

Takeaway

In this chapter, you've learned:

- What spellcasting is and how to prepare yourself before you begin.

- When a spell is necessary.

- Ingredients specific to the spells in this book.

- My thoughts on magickal timing and working backwards to customize your spell to suit the timing, with example spells.

- Why rhymes are used in most of the spells.

CHAPTER 3

Body of Protection and Circle of Banishing

The best lightning rod for your protection is your own spine.
-Ralph Waldo Emerson

These are going to be the most used protection spells you have in your arsenal. The Body of Protection can be done anytime, anywhere. It will be the shield against anything harmful that could come against you. You can make it as heavy or light as you need, reinforce it in emergencies, and add instructions to it. The basic instruction is to filter out the bad and let in the good. You can also charge it to enhance a psychic sense like clairvoyance or give you a heads up when danger is near.

The Circle of Banishing is a little more complicated, but not by much. Banishing is akin to blocking someone on social media and setting your accounts to "private." It creates a sacred space to let you do your magick in peace. This spell requires several tools, so it's best performed in a stationary place in your home. Of course, if you're away from home, you can still perform this spell. I know I would want to if I was stuck in a hotel or at a relative's house. Just imagine the tools are there and you're using them.

Body Of Protection

When I mentioned a barrier earlier, this is what I meant. All you need to cast this powerful spell is your imagination. When you feel threatened in any way, imagine your body of protection surrounding your whole aura and creating an unbreakable barrier that nothing harmful can penetrate. It's important to say "nothing harmful" because we still want the good stuff to find us. Just like the physical body needs air to breathe, the energetic body needs positive energy to thrive.

Your First Time

To begin, first sit down and think about what your barrier is going to look like. Will it have a color, texture, sound, or smell? Will it be just a bubble or take on a particular shape? When there's a storm, I place a barrier of solid earth around my entire block to protect it from lightning. If I feel threatened in public, I place a body of protection around myself in the form of a clear crystal. The prism that shines through are the good vibes that I allow. What you want yours to be is entirely up to you. What's important is that you decide and stay consistent. The repetition will make it stronger each time.

Now that you've done that, spend some time with it. Practice raising and lowering it. Remember how it feels. Notice how the air changes when you put it up. Drop it and note that change, too. Getting to know your barriers before you need to use them will make it easier to use them in an emergency. In time, they'll start putting themselves up before you know you need them. Your aura will sense bad vibes before your conscious awareness and act.

The barrier you've chosen will be your main go to, the one you automatically raise when you sense trouble. There's so much that can be done to enhance them that they become spells in themselves, so here are some examples.

Reinforcing the Body of Protection

Sometimes you need reinforcements. When you've been bombarded with bad energy all day, or if someone is deliberately sending it to you, the barrier can wear down. Usually, it doesn't mean that it was weak to begin with. Throughout the day we get tired and lose focus. It can be difficult to focus on both the mundane world and keeping your barrier in place. You can reinforce your Body of Protection in two ways.

- In an emergency, just close your eyes and imagine it growing larger around you, then brighter, then stronger.

- You can charge an object to act as an automatic reinforcer when your energy level is low—especially after a long hard day at work. Use something you have with you every day like your phone, wallet, or keys.

Advanced Reinforcements

When you've practiced for a while, you'll find it easier to raise and reinforce the Body of Protection. If you are in a dangerous situation, you can raise an army out of the barrier.

- Put up the barrier and reinforce it as much as you can.

- Take a moment to breathe and gather your strength.

- Imagine the excess slipping off to form three (or more if you wish) soldiers that stand behind you, ready to defend you.

- Repeat the reinforcement to make them stronger. Do this as many times as you feel necessary.

- If this is too exhausting for you, see chapter 9 for instructions on borrowing energy.

- These soldiers will aggressively defend you when you're in trouble. This is great for those who have to be in dangerous situations every day—law enforcement, military, cab drivers, and anyone who works with money. I hate that it's a harsh world, but it is what it is. You never know when you'll need a little extra backup.

The Spiked Barrier

You don't need an army, but you would still like a little more defense added to the Body of Protection.

- Close your eyes and imagine the barrier growing stronger until you feel it's done.

- Imagine the outer layer of your reinforced barrier forming sharp spikes all over it. These can be as big or small as you wish, as long as they cover your entire body.

- Any negative energy trying to invade your space will be shredded.

I should note that an interesting side effect to this barrier is that it gives off a *leave me alone* vibe. Don't be surprised if people tend to avoid you more than usual when you use it.

The Focus Barrier

This time, your enemy is distraction. You're running out of time and you need to finish what you're doing now.

- First, turn off all electronics (except the one you're working on, if that's your task). Lock the door and put any chores out of your mind.

- Now reinforce your barrier.

- Imagine it coming from your body to surround you and your task. It solidifies into a soundproof wall so only you and your task exist.

- Take a few deep breaths and get to work. You'll find that it was done much faster than normal with minimal interruptions.

The Decoy Barrier

If you don't want the side effect of being avoided, this Body of Protection spell gives off an inviting vibe, but leaves a defense on standby to take care of any harmful energy that invades your space.

- Reinforce the Body of Protection.

- Fill the outer layer with all the love and compassion you can muster. Imagine it glowing soft pink or lavender.

- Underneath that layer, imagine the rest of the barrier glowing bright red and pulsating with energy, ready to strike down anything harmful.

The Cooling Barrier

There's something in the air and everybody's angry. Anger and heat go hand in hand, so this cooling barrier will help calm you and those in contact with you.

- Reinforce the Body of Protection.

- Imagine the whole thing becoming a soft waterfall. It sinks down into your body and calms you.

- Anyone who crosses your path is automatically calmed down as well.

The Banishing Circle

Casting a circle will banish anything harmful from your presence. There are many ways to do this. Certain traditions have their own tools and rituals, so let me break down the steps and you can decide how complicated you want it to be.

- First, you have to decide where you're going to cast the circle. You need a clear boundary because you can't cross it once it's done. If you do, it will dissolve before its time and cause any energy you've built up to shoot around erratically. If the circle is to protect against something specific, then you're vulnerable again. I've made it sound like it's the end of the world, but it's not. Don't panic if it happens accidentally. Just cast it again.

- Now you need to cleanse the area before erecting the boundary. I prefer to use Florida Water for this. Sprinkle or spray it around the area and say, "this space is clear of all evil energies, spirits, and intentions!" Say it like you mean it. Banishing is a forceful act and it should be known that you won't put up with shenanigans.

- If you have incense, light some. It's a signal to both you and any powers that may be that it's time for magick. It also calls on the powers of air to lend some extra energy to your spell.

- If you have candles, light them for the same reason as the incense. I always have "working candles" for light and ambience. Candles call on the power of fire to lend some extra energy for your spell.

- Now it's time to draw your circle. Some witches use a wand or dagger to direct energy. If you don't have either, your finger will do. Point at the ground and follow the boundary you've decided on in a clockwise rotation. A short rhyme will tell your circle what to do and fix it in your mind, "This circle is a wall that none may breach. Until it's gone, I am out of reach."

Casting this circle before doing other spellwork not only keeps out harm, but also contains the energy of your spell. This makes it stronger until you release it by banishing the circle.

Banishing the Circle

Your spells are done and you feel safe. Now what? It's time to banish the circle so you can move around again. It also signals that you are done and any energies you've called are free to leave. If not, they'll just hang around and wreak havoc like a bored toddler.

- Take your tool or finger and move counterclockwise along the boundary, erasing it slowly. Another small chant will seal it.

- "The circle is open but protection stays. I now close all portals and doorways."

- It is customary to say something to finalize the act. "Amen," "blessed be," and "so mote it be," are popular. You don't have to do this if it doesn't sit well with you.

- Extinguish your candles and clean up. Witchcraft is a messy practice, so unless you're doing a spell that must stay put for several days, always clean up after yourself. In a sense, you're clearing the energy of that spell to make room for another later. You don't want those energies mixing or your results can be erratic at best, or worse, destructive.

Portals and Doorways

You'll notice that Banishing the Circle involves closing portals and doorways. When you practice witchcraft, you open doors to the etheric plane so you can send your energy to do its job. It's important to close these when you're done, or other things can leak through. Those parasites I mentioned earlier love open doorways. They'll hang around like they're trying to get into a nightclub. That will grab the attention of more powerful entities. Closing these after the circle also closes any you didn't know were open. If you feel that a doorway may still be open after your spell, you can perform a more official closing so that your concentration is only on that task.

- After banishing the circle, imagine big red Xs surrounding the area your circle was cast.

- See them sink into the atmosphere and say, "Any portals I've opened are now closed."

- Affirm this every time until it becomes second nature.

Closing Mirror Portals

Mirrors facing doors or other mirrors act like a revolving door. You want to either move or cleanse and close them at least once a week. If you have a spirit that seems to hang out in the bathroom, it's probably not looking for a peepshow. You just need to close the portal in your medicine cabinet mirror.

- Use a cleansing spray like Florida Water or a saltwater cleanser to wipe down the entire mirror. Imagine any lingering energy washing away. Make sure you get the whole mirror, not just the front.

- With the index finger of your writing hand, draw an X over the mirror. Imagine red light forming the X and then spreading over the entire mirror.

- Give it a moment to sink in, then use a regular cleaner to wipe off any streaks.

Likewise, if you have any crystal balls or scrying mirrors, it's best to keep them covered when not in use. These are portals specifically used to see into the etheric plane and hold more power to that effect. In the case of crystal balls, keeping them covered also prevents the sun from hitting them and causing a fire. I have a nice scar on my leg from bringing home my first crystal ball. I set it in my lap in the car and learned my lesson right then.

A Word of Advice

Magick is, in my experience, a living thing. We as witches move the magick in the direction it needs to go, but it decides how it's going to get there and how long it lasts. Be as specific as possible without limiting yourself when casting your spells. If you find that it worked but wore off quickly, just recast it and go about your business. If it worked but in an unexpected way, that's okay as long as the result didn't hurt you. Ask yourself if you could reword it for a better outcome next time. With experience, you'll get better and longer lasting results.

Don't be discouraged if a certain spell didn't work for you right away. Instantaneous magick is rare and sometimes it takes a while. Magick works quite a bit to bring you what you want. Just put it out of your mind instead of lending negativity to it. When you're in a better frame of mind, try again or try something different. Half the fun is experimenting with different spells.

Takeaway

In this chapter, you've learned:

- What the Body of Protection spell is and different ways to use it.

- Casting a Banishing Circle and Banishing the Circle spells.

- What portals and doorways are and how to close them.

- A spell for closing mirror portals.

- A word of encouragement from me.

Chapter 4

Cleansing Spells and Rituals

Wash away my troubles, wash away my pain with the rain in Shambala. Wash away my sorrow, wash away my shame with the rain in Shambala.

-Three Dog Night

What is Cleansing?

To cleanse is to get rid of any old or invasive energy. You can cleanse yourself or others, objects, and even situations. You can do a cleansing if you suspect a psychic attack, or if you're in a foul mood that you can't seem to shake. If you never liked that ring your grandma gave you even though it's beautiful, it needs cleansing.

Cleansing yourself when you get home every day not only gets the bad vibes off you, but also prevents them from clinging to anything else in your home. This is especially important if you work in the healthcare field. I've worked in nursing homes and with the developmentally disabled. Those illnesses seem to take on a life of their own. Like viruses, they will stick to you and multiply on anyone else you come into contact with.

Crystals and Stones

If you're into crystals, there's a bit of debate about cleansing them. Some say they cleanse themselves and some say they should be cleansed. I believe it's a little of both. One you get the hang of feeling out energies, you'll be able to tell if something needs cleansing. Some crystals are used especially for cleansing, so they naturally have a higher vibration.

Selenite is the most potent one I've used. You can get it in smaller pieces and add it to your charm bags, tarot boxes, or anything else you'd like to keep cleansed all the time. That can get pricey so if you don't have the money, but a once a month ritual for those things will work for you.

Clear quartz is an all-purpose stone that you can program. Cleanse it with a ritual, then charge it to work your will. The energy in these tends to get stagnant if not used regularly, so you'll need to redo the cleansing and charging once in a while.

Symbols for Cleansing

The part of the mind that works magick is the subconscious. Its language is that of symbolism and that's what makes them important in your spells and rituals. You can use established symbols like the pentacles of Solomon, find some you like online, or make your own.

Making your own symbols (called sigils in witchy circles) makes your magick unique and more powerful. Only you know what you want and how you want it to manifest. What says cleansing to you? For me, it's a rain shower. I draw up a little cloud with seven raindrops coming out of it. There are several methods to make your own sigils. It doesn't matter if you have artistic skills or not. The point is to gel it in your subconscious to bring your will in line with the goal.

Other Items for Cleansing

Both salt and water are great purifiers. Sage is commonly used, but please be aware that the sage used in those cleansing bundles you see sold everywhere is endangered. Make sure your sage is sourced ethically. Pine and juniper are also great. You can put them in a simmer pot and the steam will release cleansing throughout the house. Lemon peel can also be added.

For a cleansing bath, put these into an organza bag and fill up the tub: salt, juniper berries, pine needles, and lemon peel. I add a splash of Florida Water also. As you soak, imagine white light flowing out of the bag and through you, inside and out. Make sure to pour some over your head. This formula can also be put in a spray bottle for quick cleansing. I always use a cleansing spray right before spellwork even if I've taken my bath.

Cleansing Spells

White Light Cleansing Spell

This spell is for cleansing smaller objects like jewelry, but can be adapted for bigger items. Here we're using the power of the elements of earth, air, fire, and water for the work.

- You will need purifying incense like pine or sage, a white candle, a little dish of salt, and a little bowl of water.

- Set your items up in a circle and place the item to be cleansed in the middle. Light the incense. If you want to cast a circle, do that now.

- Light your candle and focus on what you want to accomplish for a moment.

- Take a deep breath and pick up the item. Exhale and run it through the incense smoke. Say, "With the power of air, you are cleansed." Imagine the smoke pushing white light into the object and black goo leaving.

- Run the item above the candle flame. Be careful. You only want the heat to touch it, not start a fire. Say, "With the power of fire, you are cleansed." Imagine light the color of the flame pushing into the object and black goo leaving.

- Sprinkle a small pinch of salt on the item. Say, "With the power of earth, you are cleansed." Imagine forest green energy pushing into the object and black goo leaving.

- Dip your fingers into the water and sprinkle it onto the item. Say, "By the power of water, you are cleansed." Imagine blue light pushing into the object and black goo leaving.

- To finish, breathe onto the object. The energy coming from your breath can be whatever color you wish. Say, "By the power of myself, you are cleansed!" Say it like you mean it and imagine all the rest of the black goo fleeing from the object and out of your space.

If your candle hasn't burned out, extinguish it. You can leave the incense burning unless you're going to leave. If you've cast a circle, banish it and clean up.

Mirror Spell for Cleansing

Mirror spells are most commonly used for the protection spells that you'll read about in the next chapter, but they can also be used for cleansing. Mirrors not only allow you to see into other realms and reflect negativity away from you, but they also amplify whatever spell you're doing. I found a great use for my bathroom mirror when I decided to try something different. You'll start this spell right before getting into the shower.

- You will need a small candle and some incense.

- Light these on the sink and focus on the mirror.

- See the mirror shine with bright light.

- Take your shower. When finished, stare into the foggy mirror and say, "Each time you catch my gaze, I am purified from all malaise."

- Allow the fog to dissipate naturally and imagine it sinking in to seal the spell. Now every time you look into your bathroom mirror, you will be cleansed and alert.

Home Purification

This spell is a little more involved. Just like regular cleaning, you have to get every nook and cranny. I've used it to cleanse my own home and others at a distance.

- You will need your supplies for your Circle of Banishing, plus one extra white candle.

- Cast your circle, except this time cast it around the entire house in a clockwise rotation, and pick up the extra candle. Hold it between your palm and imagine bright white light pouring from your writing hand into the candle. Say, "I cleanse this house from the unwanted and obscene. From open space to shadowed corner, this place is clean!"

- Light the candle and put it in a holder that you can carry around with you. In a clockwise direction, take the candle to shine all over your house while you chant. Open every cabinet, closet and drawer and picture the radiance of the candle flame pouring into them. If a spider can hide, so can nasty energies. Take your time with this. If you rush, you could miss something.

- If the candle is still burning when you come back around to your working space, set it down and let it burn out while you concentrate on the brilliance of the flame penetrating the entire space.

- When the candle is burned out, banish your circle and clean up.

To Purify a Situation

We've all had those days where nothing seems to go right. You're dropping everything, the wi-fi drops during an important meeting, the car has a flat when you need groceries. You get the picture. Maybe it only happens when you're focused on a particular situation. Every time you try to accomplish something (like signing up for college classes or looking for a new job), an invisible hand comes in and gives everything a good shake and you just can't seem to get there. This spell will purify the circumstances and help you with clarity so you know what steps should be taken next.

- You will need to cast a banishing circle before you begin, have your supplies on hand for that.

- For the spell, you will need a white candle and a representation of the situation to be cleansed. This can be a symbol you've drawn, a picture, or a petition you've written.

- Cast your circle then hold the candle in your hands. Say, "From (situation) all obstacles are slain. Victory is mine again and again!"

- Imagine anything blocking your success in that situation disappearing, replaced by white light. Use your picture, symbol, or petition for the image.

- Place the representation under the candle. Light the candle but keep the image in your mind as it burns.

- Allow the candle to burn out while you focus and chant.

- When it's burned all the way down, banish the circle and clean up.

Onion and Candle Cleansing

The onion is a natural vacuum for bad energy. This spell does double duty to get rid of bad energy.

- You will need an onion, a white candle, a candle holder, a bowl to put the onion in, and a knife to cut the onion.

- Hold the candle and imagine white light flowing into it through your writing hand. Say, "Nothing bad escapes your flame. Calm and content, this place is tame."

- Place the candle in its holder.

- Cut the top off the onion so its layers are exposed.

- Place it in the bowl, cut side up and hold your hands over it. Imagine a black void swirling inside the onion, ready to suck up any negative energy. Say, "Into this black hole, all malevolence goes. Forever gone and the portal's closed."

- Place the onion bowl in front of the candle.

- Light the candle and imagine all bad vibes getting sucked to the onion. If any escape, they get bounced into the candle flame to be burned away.

- Let the candle burn all the way down.

- Leave the onion out until it begins to rot.

- Don't touch it directly, but toss it in the garbage when it's done.

You can also use onions in other ways to maintain the cleansing, but it can get smelly.

- Cut onions in half and place them in the corners of your home. Change them out once a week.

- Placing halved onions on your nightstand keeps negativity and nightmares away when you're sleeping (if you can sleep with that smell).

Garlic Cleansing

Like onions, garlic can get smelly, but not as bad. I prefer garlic to onions because not only are they powerful cleansers, but also protectors.

- You can add garlic powder to any herbal mixture that involves cleansing or protection. This includes incense blends and herbal baths. You only need a pinch to do the trick.

- Whole garlic slices can be placed in the corners of your home and on windowsills to create a boundary. Anyone or anything that comes into your home is automatically cleansed.

- Add a pinch of garlic to your cleansing water to sprinkle around your home. It will give it an enormous boost.

The Magick of Sound

Certain sounds are also powerful cleansing agents. They emit certain frequencies and raise the vibes around them that negativity finds inhospitable.

- Singing bowls emit a high frequency continuous pitch that's like nails on chalkboard for negative vibes and malevolent spirits. When you bump the side of the bowl with the mallet, it will break up the bad vibe. I like to bump-sing-bump when cleansing to scatter the bad energy, then push it out, then scatter again to get my point across.

- Like the bump of the singing bowl, tambourines, gongs, and rattles break up stubborn vibes so they can be cleared away. After you've given them a good shake throughout your space, perform your preferred cleansing. You'll find that it's much easier now.

Bells

Bells have a long history in witchcraft. They break up and scare away bad energy, leaving your home automatically clean and protected. Often, they are placed on doorknobs so nothing can get through these revolving thresholds, but there are several ways you can use bells to suit you.

- Ring the bell throughout your space as you would the above tools. Perform a cleansing afterward and reinforce your boundary.

- Keep three small bells on a keychain or purse for cleansing and protection when you're out of the home.

- Keep a small bell with your circle supplies to quickly get rid of nosy entities.

- If you're into hair braids like me, you can attach small jingle bells to your hair. This scatters anything directed at your mind—controlling spells, love spells, and outside emotions. Just have a way to silence them if you work in a quiet setting.

Distance Cleansing

Cleansing spells can be used for anything, even at a distance. You can tailor any of these spells to work for someone far away just as well as yourself.

- All you need is a representation of the person—a taglock, name paper, or even poppet.

- Perform your cleansing on the representation as you would if they were standing before you.

- Cleansing leaves a blank slate. You should do a blessing of protection from the next chapter when you're through.

Takeaway

In this chapter, you've learned:

- A white light cleansing spell.

- A mirror spell for cleansing.

- A home purification spell.

- A spell to purify a situation.

- An onion and candle cleansing spell.

- A garlic cleansing spell.

- How sound can be used for cleansing.

- How to use bells in cleansing.

- A distance cleansing spell.

CHAPTER 5

Protection Spells

In moments of great uncertainty in my travels, I have always felt that something is protecting me, that I will come to no harm.

-Tahir Shah

This is what we're here for. You can do a protection spell for anything. Some of them require a few tools and some of them only require your desire and imagination. If you are a beginner, you should know that protection spells don't work like they do in fiction. No spells do. They must have an avenue to manifest the spell. For example, if you do a safe travel spell and end up broken down on the highway, you may be angry and think the spell didn't work. Then you see a state police car speeding past you with lights and sirens blaring. There was a major collision ahead caused by a drunk driver. Your spell worked perfectly. This happened to me once, and I've never doubted again.

Before You Cast

If you need protection from something specific, do a reading to make sure you're on the right path. It does no good to guard against a bear when there's a snake under your feet.

Unless it's an emergency, you should always do a cleansing first. Clear out all the bad vibes and prevent more from invading.

Not everything from the spirit world is evil. In fact, I've run across more nosy ghosts than malevolent entities. If you're not sure, do a reading. Scry if that's your talent. It could even be a spirit guide that's trying to give you advice. A witch should get to know the spirit world and its inhabitants, even if they don't use them for their spells.

A protection spell can be done any time it's needed. You don't need a specific date, time, or moon phase. These are correspondences that make your spellwork more potent, but aren't necessary.

Home Protection

Our home is supposed to be our sanctuary. It is imperative that we feel safe in the place where we sleep. Bad things happen even in the best of neighborhoods, and a physical or spiritual home invasion is a nightmare. Lock your doors, get a doorbell camera, and practice these spells.

Protective Boundary Spell

- You will need supplies to cast a circle, salt, red pepper, black pepper, and a bowl to mix them together. A utensil for mixing is advisable if you don't want to get hot pepper under your nails. Mixing with your hands does lend more power to the spell, though. The choice is yours.

- Cast your circle. Pour some salt into the bowl. Place your writing hand over the bowl and imagine bright red light saturating the salt (red is a Mars color, hence my use for protection instead of love). Say, "I charge you to create a perfect boundary of protection."

- Add the black pepper into the bowl. Place your writing hand over the bowl and imagine bright red light saturating the pepper. Say, "I charge you to create a perfect boundary of protection."

- Add the red pepper into the bowl. Place your writing hand over the bowl and imagine bright red light saturating the pepper. Say, "I charge you to create a perfect boundary of protection."

- Stir the ingredients while you imagine them glowing with that red light. Say, "As I stir this potion round and 'bout, no harm in and all harm out!"

- Sprinkle this powder along the baseboards of your home. Remember, a little goes a long way. Make sure you go all around the home while imagining a bright red wall going up, sprinkle by sprinkle. Say, "I build a wall with this charm. This wall is a fortress against all harm!"

- Banish the circle and clean up. If there's leftover powder, put it in a well-sealed canister and label it for next time. If you feel the boundary has dissipated, repeat the last step.

The Gargoyle Sentry

Gargoyles have a long history of protecting a place. I got a tiny novelty gargoyle as a gift and the idea hit me. He would make a perfect protection talisman.

- You'll need a small gargoyle statue for this one. They can be bought online for reasonable prices. It can even be hollow plastic or a stuffed toy. It's the symbolism of the gargoyle that matters. You're going to make a thoughtform (programmed energy) to live in the gargoyle and defend your home.

- Have your circle supplies ready, crystals if you have any, and a couple of extra candles. You will need the extra energy for this spell.

- Cast the circle and ask for the aid of the elements and cosmos. Imagine their energies swirling and mixing all around you. Raise your own energy by dancing, chanting, rubbing your hands together, or all the above.

- When you can't do it anymore, imagine the energy becoming more dense and powerful until it forms the shape of your gargoyle. It can be any size you wish, it doesn't have to match the statue.

- Now you have to tell your gargoyle what to do. I simply tell it, "Your job is to protect this home and all within it. Protect this home and all within it. Protect this home and all within it." Repeat this until you feel it's properly programmed.

- Now pick up the statue and hold it up to your thoughtform and tell it, "This is where you rest and recharge." Imagine the thoughtform going into the statue like a genie in a bottle. It will automatically come out and defend your home if it's needed.

- The spell is done (for now). Banish your circle and clean up.

You need to feed your gargoyle regularly. Thoughtforms need infusions of energy to sustain themselves. You can surround it with crystals, light candles beside it, breathe your own energy into it, or set it up on a window to soak up both sun and moon powers. Wherever you put it, make sure you can see it everyday and thank it for protecting you. If you forget about it, it will work for a while but eventually dissipate or go elsewhere. It needs both food and attention to work for you.

Now you have your very own gargoyle sentry to defend your space, its people, and pets. You made it from your own power with the assistance of other energies. That means it can do no harm to you nor disobey. Once in a great while, thoughtforms can be erratic because of energy overload. If it gets out of control, just demand that it dissipate and take away its energy sources.

Personal Protection Spells

Personal protection spells don't mean invincibility. Sometimes they prevent bad things from happening, and other times they give you the tools to deal with your problem. If you fall down the stairs because you weren't paying attention, maybe you just sprain your ankle instead of breaking your leg in three places. If you feel a psychic attack, a protection spell will have a banishing element to it, pushing away the invading energy.

Your Personal Flamethrower

When a standard Body of Protection will not do, it's time to get out your Flamethrower.

This is anything that lights. A candle, match, lighter, or actual torch is what we have in mind. If you're in the comfort of your own home, a candle will do. I use a lighter because it's a portable charm and no one would know I'm casting a spell with it.

- You will need your circle supplies and a lighter that you can dedicate to this protection spell.

- Cast the circle and pick up the lighter.

- Pass it through the incense and say, "By the power of air, I cleanse and charge you as my protective flamethrower."

- Pass it over the heat of the candle flame and say, "By the power of fire, I cleanse and charge you as my protective flamethrower."

- Sprinkle a pinch of salt over it and say, "By the power of earth, I cleanse and charge you as my protective flamethrower."

- Dip your fingers into the water and sprinkle it over the lighter. Say, "By the power of water I cleanse and charge you as my protective flamethrower."

- Breathe onto the lighter and say, "By the power of my breath, I cleanse and charge you as my protective flamethrower."

- Cup the lighter in your hands and send bright red light

into it with your writing hand. Say, "A wall of fire surrounds me now. Nothing crosses except what I allow!"

- Give it a try. Light it and picture the flame shooting out to surround you. When you're done, you can just imagine it sinking into the earth to extinguish the flame.

- Banish your circle and clean up.

You now have a personal flamethrower that you can take with you anywhere. You can use it in addition to the Body of Protection or by itself.

Protect Your Finances

You can protect your wallet, purse, billfold, or digital wallet from being lost or stolen. We've probably all had it happen. The wallet wiggles its way out of your pocket. Your purse gets left at the coffee shop. Someone swipes your data from a phone application. This spell prevents that from happening. Just don't set your purse down in public.

- You'll need your circle supplies and wallet, purse, or phone—anything that has money in it.

- Cast the circle. Put your objects inside the circle of water, salt, incense, and candle.

- This time you're going to imagine the power of the elements swirling around and through them, with earth being first and last. Earth is the element of finances, so I like to put a double whammy on this spell.

- Say, "My money is mine to do as I please. It shall not fall into the hands of some random sleaze."

- Repeat this over and over until you feel done. You'll know when to quit. If you're not sure, keep going.

- Banish the circle and clean up. Your money is protected. You should repeat this spell anytime you have new money come in, whether it's a paycheck, winnings, or birthday gift.

Travel Safety

Traveling comes with its own set of dangers. When you're in unknown territory, you don't know who the people are, or are not used to the environment, your adventure could quickly turn sour. The mode of transportation doesn't matter. This spell is for you, not a vehicle. We'll cover that in the next section. This is a personal protection spell that covers you and your belongings.

- You will only need your desire and imagination for this. It's a supercharged form of the Body of Protection spell.

- Put up your Body of Protection. Make sure that it surrounds you and everything on you—luggage, for example. Imagine a brick wall building itself around that. This is more difficult than it sounds. You may want to practice before you need to use it. Make this wall as tangible as you can. Hear the bricks stacking, see a little dust fly up. Your nervousness about being in unknown territory is what gives this extra power.

- If you need a cue, you can say or think, if you're in a crowd of people, "I am safe from all seen and unseen dangers."

- Since this is tied to your nervous energy, it will naturally dissipate when you feel safe and relaxed again.

Why not use this all the time instead of the standard Body of Protection? You certainly can, but it takes a lot of extra energy to maintain. Plus, it's like using a fortress with a moat and gun turrets to guard against a baby mouse.

Magickal Stain Repellent

This one is super easy and fun. It prevents any minor annoyances from sticking to you. It's great if you have a stressful day ahead.

- Keep up the Body of Protection and add a slippery layer on top of it. I like to imagine mine coated with dish soap because it's slippery and cleansing.

- Make sure to take it down when you get home. All you

have to do is will it to disappear. Unlike the standard Body of Protection, this one doesn't allow any external energy through, good or bad.

Protection Sigils

Sigils have become very popular and there's a reason for it. They're easy to make and very powerful when enough energy is put into them. There are several ways to make a sigil and that can fill a whole book or three. For the purposes of this spell, we'll use the pentagram.

- Draw a pentacle (a five pointed star with a circle around it) on a piece of paper.

- Put the paper where you can see it easily and focus on it. Relax enough that your eyes go slightly out of focus.

- Repeat the simple statement, "I am protected."

- Don't break your focus. The symbol will eventually flash or disappear for a split second. It's charged when it does.

- Keep it with you for an added barrier.

Object Protection

We all have things we'd like to protect more than others. Cars, heirlooms, and such. In my case, books love to disappear on me, so I cast a protection on my favorites.

Simple Object Protection

- Hold your hands over the item and imagine bright red light going into it.

- Say, "You are protected from getting lost or stolen, damaged or broken."

Vehicle Charm

I didn't forget. Here is the spell for your transportation, whatever form that takes.

- You will need your circle supplies and a charm to hang from your vehicle. It can be anything from a pendant to a charm specifically made for the rearview mirror. I was lucky enough to find one in the shape of a crescent moon with stars dangling from it. A protective symbol is a plus—a cross, pentacle, or rune—but it's not necessary.

- Cast the circle.

- Run the charm through the incense and say, "I cleanse you with the power of air."

- Hold it over the candle flame at a safe distance and say, "I cleanse you with the power of fire."

- Sprinkle a pinch of salt over it and say, "I cleanse you with the power of earth."

- Sprinkle a few drops of water over it and say, "I cleanse you with the power of water."

- Hold the charm with your writing hand over it. Send bright red energy into it.

- Instead of rhyme, repetition will seal the spell. Say, "From breakdowns and accidents, this vehicle is protected. From empty gas tanks and flat tires, this vehicle is protected. From any danger at all, this vehicle is protected!"

- Repeat this and keep pushing that energy into the charm until you feel done.

- Your charm is ready to place in (or on) your mode of transportation. If you start feeling nervous on the road, just glance at the charm and repeat the chant.

- Banish the circle and clean up.

Heirloom Protection

I have left spirits out of this book so far because I want you to customize it to your own beliefs. If you want to protect something that was handed down in the family, then asking your ancestors to lend a hand will make that protection extra powerful.

- You will need your circle supplies, an extra candle to dedicate to your ancestors, and the heirloom. If you're calling a specific family member that you knew in life, having a few things that they liked on your workspace will help bring them to you.

- Cast the circle. Cleanse the candle and heirloom.

- Hold the candle in both hands and close your eyes. Breathe for a few moments and focus on contacting your departed relatives. When done, place the candle in its holder.

- Light the candle and hold the heirloom like it's the most sacred thing you've ever touched.

- Say, "I call on my ancestors (name any if using specific relatives) to help me protect this (name the heirloom), which was passed down to my care. Keep it safe until it's my turn to pass it down."

- If it's small enough, lay the object in front of the candle. Make sure it's safe from dripping wax.

- Sit and close your eyes while the candle burns. If you wish, you can chant the call to your ancestors, or can meditate on bringing them to help you.

- When the candle has burned out, banish the circle and

clean up.

Make sure to thank your ancestors and put the heirloom away in a safe place.

Protecting Others

The main reason I got into protection spells was for my baby. He's growing up fast, but I still want to keep him safe his whole life. I'm sure every parent would love to lock their kids away and shield them from the world, but that's a little psychotic. Instead, we can protect them with our magick and give them their freedom bit by bit until they're ready to fly the nest.

Protect your child when they're away

- You'll need your circle supplies, a picture of your child, and a red candle.

- Cast your circle.

- Hold both the candle and picture, imagining bright red light flowing into them from your writing hand.

- Place the candle where you can prop the picture up in front of it.

- Light the candle, stare into the picture, and say, "Protected be, protected be, from harm or injury. With this candle flame, I protect my baby!"

- Keep chanting while you imagine the power of the candle funneling through the picture to your child until it burns out.

- Banish your circle and clean up.

No matter how old they are, your kids will always be your babies. Keep them as safe as possible for as long as you can.

Blessing of Protection

Have you ever met someone and felt an overwhelming desire to protect them? Maybe you had a bad feeling as soon as you shook hands, or maybe this person was in obvious distress. I came up with this little spell when I met a scared young homeless woman. I had nothing to give her except some magick.

- Imagine the person surrounded in white light, which in turn is surrounded by red light.

- Say (if only in your head), "I bless you with the protection of my magick."

That's it. Simple but powerful. This spell will wear off after a few hours, but it's perfect to help someone you're not closely connected to.

Sealed with a Kiss

For those who you are closely connected to like your spouse, kids, or great aunt who won't let you pass by without a kiss, this spell is great for automatic protection for you and those you love.

- All you need is some lip balm.

- Hold it in your hands and send the red light into it.

- Say, "Perfect protection for all you touch."

- Repeat this until you feel done.

Lip balm is a fantastic gender neutral item you can keep on you. Every time you kiss someone, an added layer of protection will surround them.

Now you have plenty of protection spells for your arsenal. Any one of these can be customized for your specific situation.

Takeaway

In this chapter, you've learned:

- Things to do before you cast a spell.

- A protective boundary spell.

- A gargoyle sentry spell.

- A personal flamethrower spell.

- A spell to protect your finances.

- A spell for travel safety.

- A magickal stain repellent spell.

- Protection sigils.

- A simple object protection spell.

- A vehicle charm spell.

- An heirloom protection spell.

- A spell to protect your child.

- A blessing of protection spell.

- A lip balm enchantment to protect those you kiss.

CHAPTER 6

Curses

Regarding war and peace—the seeds of each are planted in the other.

-Clifford Cohen

There are many debates regarding cursing. Some say it should never be done. Some say it should be done often. I'm the type of person who thinks that even if you don't do it, you should at least know how to curse. It's like having a gun in your house for self-defense. Keep it locked away and know how to use it properly so you don't hurt yourself. You should also study the types of curses that are popular and their effects. This will help you diagnose yourself and others, and give you a better idea on what to protect against.

Types of Curses

There are many shady people in the world. With the internet

and e-book explosion, you can find a curse for everything. A lot of them go in canisters for some reason. Some use poppets, sigils, or long involved rituals. There are curses to give you bad luck, ill health, and even death. There are those who would see you lose all your friends and family, so they'll work to isolate you from them. Then there are those who want to dominate you sexually. Magickal rape. It's really a thing. Some people are just control freaks who want to get their way, so they'll do persuasion magick on you. Some are just envious souls who can throw a good evil eye (intentional or not).

It seems like everybody wants their ex back. The market is dominated with this type of curse. Again, it's magickal rape. It often comes with a separation spell for the ex and their current partner. Spells to get your ex back are not love spells! Like physical rape, they are about control and obsession. That isn't love. Why would anyone want to force someone back into a failed relationship? If you suspect that someone has done this or paid someone to do this to you, reinforce your Body of Protection immediately. Then either do a reading or have a reading done to confirm. If you know who it is, banish them from your life. If you don't, work extra hard on your protection spells until they give up. Remember, predators like easy prey.

In chapter two I discussed diagnosing curses and other forms of bad influences. I want to repeat here that a lot of these could be signs of medical conditions, so please see a doctor. That being said, many curses take the form of medical conditions, so it's both. Have the conditions treated by a medical professional and do your curse breaking spells.

One thing I noticed about curses is that if they are strong enough, they will be carried in by a sudden infestation of bugs. This is a way to give the curse a physical form so it can bypass magickal protection. If you've never had a bug problem in your home and suddenly it's covered in fleas (and you don't even have pets), you need to do a reading right then. Chances are, someone has decided that you're an enemy.

Along with the infestations, you'll start to notice your home or vehicles start to fall into disrepair. You have a flat, then the bathroom begins to spew sewage everywhere, then the alternator goes out and you have to have your car towed. Your roof starts leaking and a tree branch busts a window. It'll be one thing after another, like dominoes.

Magick isn't good or bad. It just is. It's the people wielding it that are good or bad. The magickal community is as diverse as the rest of the world and it's up to you to decide what kind of witch you want to be.

Family Curses

Family curses, also called generational curses, can be disheartening. These are curses that span several lifetimes in your genetic history. There's not much you can do about them except develop a thick skin and be more on guard. You will have to work twice as hard to keep up with your cleansing and protection. They can be caused by any number of things in your family's past. Someone may have crossed the wrong person, trespassed on sacred land, or witnessed something they shouldn't have.

Signs of a family curse include self-hatred, depression, bad luck from birth, being prone to freak accidents, and inability to move ahead in life no matter how hard you try. Look into your past and see if any older family members had the same problems. Sometimes it skips a generation or two, and it usually affects only one or two members a generation.

If you have determined that a family curse is upon you, you can ward yourself against its effects.

- First, if you have any heirlooms, cleanse them thoroughly.

- You will need your circle supplies and a light blue candle.

- Cast the Banishing Circle and pick up the blue candle.

- Send blue light into it and say, "I am not my bloodline, and my bloodline is not me. You are fully healed and can now set me free."

- Light the candle and imagine the anger behind the curse

melting away. Now see the light blue coating your aura and Body of Protection.

- Let the candle burn out.

- Banish the circle and clean up.

Light blue is the color of healing and calmness, so this spell is meant to remove the rage that drives such a powerful curse. If any gets past it, the Body of Protection will stop it.

This spell isn't one that you do only once. You will have to renew it at least once a month until the threat is gone.

The Curse of Social Media

Everybody's online these days. It's both a blessing and a curse. The blessing is that everyone is more connected than ever. The curse is that everyone is more connected than ever—friends, family, enemies, and strangers. Anyone can get your picture along with your name and birthday now. People just decide they hate you for no other reason than to have something to argue about. It was different when circles were small and pictures hard to come by. What's a witch to do about this new threat?

- A spider's web is a symbol of networking, but it's also a symbol of trapping insects (or internet trolls). Make a simple spider web symbol to put on all your devices that have internet access. I specifically start with an asterisk and then draw the curved lines for the web.

- You can make your own stickers, or just draw them on with a marker.

- Gather your devices in one place and hold your hands over them.

- Imagine silver energy flowing into the symbols and say, "I am not my picture and my picture is not me. No taglocks of mine exist online. All curses let me be."

- Imagine the spider's web trapping any negative energy coming from your electronics.

- This should be renewed at least every three months.

Freeze that Curse

Perhaps you know who is cursing you. Maybe they straight up told you it was them. I've known more than a few cocky jerks in my time. They all think they're so powerful that nothing can touch them. They want to breed fear and thrive on conflict. They need to chill, and you can make that happen.

- You will need a small container with a locking lid. I get mine from the dollar store. If you have a taglock (something containing the person's DNA), all the better, but you can use their name and picture.

- Hold the taglock in your hands and think of the person. Say, "I name you (name). You are (name)." Imagine the item connecting to the person through a silver cord of energy.

- Put the taglock into the container and cover it with water. Close it up and say, "Frozen, frozen, locked away. Your spell against me cannot stay!"

- Put the container in the back of your freezer. Imagine an iceberg crawling up the person as the water freezes. When it's frozen solid, the culprit can do no harm.

- Take a cleansing bath afterward to knock off all remaining traces of the curse and put up the Body of Protection.

The Reversal

This is a popular spell and there are specialty candles and oils available. Some grocery stores even carry seven day glass candles for reversing. Should you use them?

I have seen debate within the community. Some say it's a curse in the guise of a protection spell. Others say that one shouldn't take responsibility for someone else's evil. The reversal spell is simply a way to make that person take on their own malevolent vibes. I'm with the latter. It's not your energy, why should you have to be responsible for it?

- You will need your circle supplies. You don't want curse energy bombarding you while trying to do this spell.

- You can get one of those special reversing candles if you like, but I just use a candle on top of a small mirror. I prefer black, but it's not a necessity.

- Cast the circle.

- Pick up the candle and imagine your favorite color of light going into the candle. The idea is that the curse be drawn to the candle and not you.

- Say, "It's missed the mark, you have bad aim. This curse returns from whence it came!"

- Affix the candle to the mirror and light it.

- Repeat the chant until the candle burns out. This may take a while and you may get bored, but keep going.

- While you chant, imagine the energy of the curse getting sucked into the candle. It shoots out the flame and the mirror directs it back where it belongs.

- Banish the circle and clean up.

Heavy Duty Curse Breaker

This is one simple ingredient you can get at a dollar store—ammonia. Maybe I should have put it in the cleansing section, but I wanted to put it here because it has an explosive effect on curse energy.

- You will need some ammonia in a spray bottle.

- Spray and wipe down walls, windows, doorways, and mirrors.

- It helps to imagine you are wiping the slate clean, popping in tiny explosions as it hits malevolent vibes.

It works on its own. You don't have to do a spell for it. In fact, you shouldn't. Ammonia destroys *all* magickal energy, including yours. Make sure you don't have any spells going when attempting this. I only use it in dire emergencies. Be careful not to get it on yourself, especially in your eyes. You may have to work in sections so you can get some fresh air. The fumes are horrible.

Curse Annulment

If you're not in a fighting mood or don't know who's sending the curse, there's still something you can do. It's not hard to do and you don't need any supplies. If you've got the Body of Protection down, you can do this.

- You feel curse energy coming at you like cannon fire. You've put up your Body of Protection, but you still feel it. Extend that field so that it actively catches the energy.

Pull it to the ground, which absorbs and recycles it.

- You don't have to say anything, but I find that appropriate hand movements are helpful.

- Take a cleansing bath to wash away all remnants of the curse and reinforce your Body of Protection.

For the most part, a person will send a curse at you and forget about it, so this is enough. Be vigilant, though. If it's someone you see every day or someone who follows your social media accounts, they will watch to make sure it took. If they feel you're not miserable enough, they will send another curse.

Witch Wars

We have got to stop lobbing curses at one another like water balloons. There are bigger threats out there and our petty squabbling can have some serious consequences. Did you know that there are crazy people out there who still believe burning and hanging witches is the thing to do? These folks have followers, and lots of them! If all of us would just call a truce, protect against the real threats, and focus on our individual successes, then we would be much happier witches. If everyone is well protected, then it would be pointless to curse each other all the time. That's why I decided to write this book.

If you decide that war is the only way to end your suffering or the suffering of others, then I have a bit of advanced magick for you. It's advanced because it requires lots of concentration and imagination, but the only tool required is you.

- First, you're going to have to build your confidence. Play some music that makes you feel powerful and strong.

- Make sure you won't be disturbed for a while.

- Reinforce your Body of Protection.

- Get comfortable and close your eyes.

- Breathe deeply and slowly, but stay comfortable.

- Relax and close your eyes.

- Imagine you can see nothing but energy waves of all different colors around you. After you study them for a moment, you can tell them apart. Some are coming from your body, stretching out until they disappear in the distance. The ones that connect to spells you have cast are in the corresponding colors of those spells. That means they are still working for you. There will be one or more that are thick and the color of swirling blacklight. See it with a worm-like mouth attached to your barrier, trying to corrupt it.

- Brace yourself and grab it. It will be slippery, but get a good hold on it and start pulling. This may take a while and serious focus, but eventually, you will pull the person who cast the curse to you. You may only see their aura and barrier and not a physical shape.

- Once you have them close, grab the curse tendril by the head and yank it out of your barrier. It may hurt, but you can repair any damage later.

- Wrap the tendril around your attacker until they are completely covered.

- Attach the head of it to the culprit's barrier and push them away. They should fall out of sight.

- When you're done, open your eyes and move around a bit.

- Do a cleansing right away and reinforce your Body of Protection, imagining any damage repaired.

This is a drastic form of reversal that cuts through all the red tape. You get to face your attacker and kick the crap out of them.

One Last Thought

If you think you are cursed, you are. Not because someone is flinging magick at you, but because victim mentality gets in its own way. You are drowning in the destructive energy that you send to yourself. This is another reason that learning a form of divination is important. The moment that you feel like someone is after you, do a reading. It will tell you definitively whether a curse is at work. Either way, do a cleansing and protection for yourself.

There are several things you can do to prevent self-cursing.

- Your words are indicators of your thought patterns. If they are mostly negative, do your best to change them. For example, if you get stopped at a red light, are running late, and always say, "Just my luck!" Then you pout until it turns green. Chances are that you will run into more red lights because it's just your luck. Try saying, "Oh well. Maybe next time," and let it go. You'll see that you've got more green lights than red.

- If you find yourself constantly stressed, you need to find some time for yourself to find inner peace. This could mean practicing yoga or meditation, walking through a park, or knitting a blanket. As long as it's something that you find relaxing to help you decompress.

- The curse breaking spells in this book aren't only for outside work. Adjust your spell to break any curses you may have placed upon yourself.

Takeaway

In this chapter, you've learned:

- The types of curses and how to diagnose them.

- How to cleanse a family curse.

- How to remove yourself from your social media photos.

- How to freeze a curse.

- How to reverse a curse.

- A heavy duty curse breaker spell.

- A curse annulment spell.

- How to deal with witch wars.

- Information on avoiding self-curses.

CHAPTER 7

Psychic Attacks and Harmful Spirits

The commonest form of psychic attack is that which proceeds from the ignorant or malignant mind of our fellow human beings.

-Dion Fortune

Psychic Attacks

Psychic attacks come from witches and regular folks. People are so hung up on their own misery that they can't stand to see anyone succeed. Just because someone doesn't practice witchcraft, that doesn't mean that their mind and aura aren't strong. If someone has decided to hate you for no reason, it's probably because they want to keep you beneath them. While it's easy to counter once you're aware, they often take you by surprise and that's their advantage.

Identifying a Psychic Attack

You could be under a psychic attack if you:

- Have no history of mental illness but suddenly start experiencing intense mood swings.

- Feel like you're being watched.

- Experience a sudden run of bad luck, especially when it seems like everything was going so well.

- Find yourself isolated from friends and family without realizing when or how it happened.

- Have sudden onset headaches and nausea each time you plan something positive.

If it goes on long enough without proper cleansing and protection, the psychic attack could fester into a curse, leading to a rapid decline in health, your home and work life completely falling apart, or something else going horribly wrong.

Like I said before, these are not definitive. Sometimes life just happens. Make sure you do your divination or have a reading done for you if you're not proficient yet.

Spell to Deflect Psychic Attack

- You will need your circle supplies and imagination. You should take a cleansing bath before you begin.

- Cast the circle.

- Reinforce your Body of Protection.

- Sit in your circle and concentrate on covering your aura and Body of Protection with mirrors. The mirrors deflect psychic attack back to the sender.

- Meditate on this until you can see and feel the mirrors covering your whole body. If at any time you feel it falter, just imagine it going back into place.

Sleep Sachet

We are most vulnerable to psychic attacks in our sleep, so a protection sachet to keep by your bed will protect you from invaders.

- You will need a small organza bag, some red pepper, and lavender.

- Fill the bag with lavender and add a pinch of the pepper.

- Hold the bag and push bright red light into it. Say, "No invasions while I sleep, all my secrets are mine to keep. This charm protects me where I lay, all ill wishes must stay away!"

- Keep the sachet on your nightstand or somewhere near your pillow. I don't recommend putting it under your pillow since it does have a pinch of red pepper in it.

Soul Enemies

Everyone has heard of soul mates, even if you don't believe in reincarnation. If you do believe, remember that everything is a balance. There is a flip side to the soul mate concept. It is possible to go through life constantly fighting a particular soul. Maybe you're always running from them, or they're running from you. Either way, it's a toxic relationship and needs to be cut away.

- You will need your circle supplies and a knife for symbolic cutting.

- Cast a circle three times. This is a psychic operation as you will be extra vulnerable.

- Relax and close your eyes. Imagine you and the other person standing face to face.

- Once that is clear, find the cord that connects you to each other. Since this is a connection that spans lifetimes, it will be thicker than normal energetic cords. It will come into focus as you concentrate on finding it. Sometimes they're in the heart area, sometimes the forehead, and sometimes they're found someplace unexpected. Scan both yours and the other person's entire bodies.

- When you've found it, make cutting motions over the area as close to your aura as possible. This is more difficult than it sounds and may take several passes.

- You will feel when the cord is free. Stay relaxed and keep the flat of the blade in front of the area. That cord will try to reattach itself more than once before it goes away, so make sure it just hits that blade.

- When it's gone, the vision of the other person and the cord will disappear.

- This will leave your aura damaged, so do a cleansing and reinforce it so it can heal without interruption.

- Banish the circle and clean up.

Protective Salt Glow

A simple beauty routine can be turned into a powerful ward against psychic attacks. It's especially useful against the evil eye of random strangers you pass by.

- You will need salt, olive oil, a bowl and utensil for mixing, and an empty jar for storage. It's good to have some on hand so you don't have to go through this process once a month.

- Mix the salt and oil into the bowl until you have a nice exfoliating consistency. The proportions are up to you.

- Pick up the bowl and place your writing hand over it. Imagine bright red light flowing into it from your palm. Say, "No ill intentions or evil thoughts. They fly away and then get lost."

- Imagine all outside influences sliding around you and darting away. Spend a while on this while chanting.

- Put the mixture in the jar and seal the lid.

- When you're ready to use it, pour some onto a wet washcloth. Gently exfoliate yourself from head to toe while chanting the rhyme. Imagine it soaking in with the olive oil.

- Get in the shower and rinse off. Be careful not to fall!

- This should last about a month, provided you keep up the Body of Protection, which reinforces it.

The Magick of Lavender

Speaking of beauty routines, this spell only requires products you may already have, or can get easily. Lavender is a wonderful flower with multiple uses. It's cleansing, protective, enhances beauty, and helps to open your third eye.

- You will need lavender scented body wash and lotion.

- Open the lids on both and hold your hands over the tops.

- Imagine bright purple energy flowing into the bottles and say, "From all attacks on my mind, I am protected. From all invasions on my aura, I am protected. By the power of lavender, I am protected!"

- When you've poured all the power you can into the bottles, cap them and use them normally. The scent and rubbing motions activate the power.

Boost Your Psychic Powers

If you're running late and forget your morning protection, how will you know if someone is throwing bad thoughts your way? Most people don't realize it until much later, after they've analyzed the signs and symptoms. This herbal sachet will boost your psychic senses so you can see (or feel) it coming and take care of it before it attaches itself to you.

- You will need a small sachet bag, salt, star anise (either whole or crushed), lavender, a bowl for mixing, and a utensil if you don't want to mix with your fingers. The proportions are up to you.

- Add the salt, star anise, and lavender to the bowl.

- Pick up the bowl and start mixing. Imagine bright purple light flowing from you to the herbs as you mix. Say, "I have the power to see through all ill intentions and lies. Nothing harmful can escape my eyes."

- Mix and chant until you're sure you've put enough energy into it.

- Pour it into the sachet and tie it closed.

- Hold it up to your nose and take a big whiff. That is the smell of psychic power.

- Carry it with you.

You can take it out and sniff it when you feel you need a boost, but it does the work on its own. If you smell it suddenly (maybe you don't even have it on you), that's a signal that protection is needed. Act accordingly.

Harmful Spirits

Spirit is a broad term. The spirit world is as diverse as the physical world. There are good and bad spirits just like there are good and bad people. It's difficult for us to tell the difference sometimes. Most people jump to the conclusion that a spirit is automatically bad if it's making its presence known. This is a mistake. Some spirits can be very helpful to your witchcraft practice and shouldn't be shunned. Gods, fairies, ancestors, spirit guides, ascended masters, animal spirits, land spirits, and friendly ghosts are a few that help the witch navigate the etheric plane.

On the other hand, there are malevolent ghosts, demonic entities, and astral parasites. Believe it or not, I have found astral parasites to be more of a nuisance than any of the others.

Astral Parasites

What makes these so bad is that they're hard to get rid of, just like a physical parasite. The more protective energy you put into it, the more it feeds until the energy is drained, so standard spells won't work. I have found that sound works best for these critters.

- You will need either a singing bowl or tambourine. I have found that a singing bowl works best for this, but these can be pricey. A tambourine is easier to come by, as even a toy one will work.

- If you like, burn some incense and a candle to get you in the mood, but this is optional.

- If you're using a singing bowl, just sit comfortably and start playing it. If you're using a tambourine, stand and shake it all around your body.

- Imagine the sound vibrating your aura so much that the parasites fly off like disturbed mosquitoes.

- See them leaving your home and going far away before reinforcing your Body of Protection.

Malevolent Ghosts

If someone was evil in life, chances are they're evil in death. A serial killer isn't going to become a saint just because he's dead. That's the real reason that playing with a spirit board is dangerous. Most people set one up and ask for any spirit to talk to them. The proper way to use this tool is to bless the board and call a guardian for it, a spirit that acts as a sort of operator— and call someone specific to speak with. The guardian won't let anyone come through who doesn't belong. Here are a few ways to deal with these pesky guys.

- Don't be afraid. Any type of harmful spirit feeds on fear. Fear generates a lot of energy and that makes them stronger. Most of what they do is only to create more fear so they can sustain themselves.

- You can't just shoo them away. You have to establish dominance. Get angry. Tell them they have to leave. Cuss and yell at them. If they're not strong enough, they will usually leave. They're looking for people they can scare, and you need to establish that it won't work with you.

- Once you've chased them away, do a cleansing from chapter four.

- When that's done, move right into creating a boundary around your home from chapter five.

Dead Roommate Spell

Maybe you're sure you have a ghost, but you're not sure if it's harmful. You don't mind it hanging around if it doesn't try to scare you or your family. This spell is to set limits for your guest without completely banishing it.

- You will need your circle supplies.

- Cast the Banishing Circle. You will use this to raise your power and protect you while you speak to the ghost.

- Tell it, "You can stay as long as you do nothing to frighten or harm anyone here. If you do, you will be banished!"

- Sit in quiet contemplation for a while. Listen for your guest. It may speak to you, give a noise as an indicator of agreement, or you will feel an affirmation.

- If everything gets still and you feel nothing, this is a sign that it doesn't agree. Start a banishing spell immediately.

Land Spirits

Land spirits, also called genius loci, reside over certain areas. Have you ever noticed that the next town feels completely different from your hometown? Even city neighborhoods have noticeable energetic boundaries. Each area has a spirit that has a symbiotic relationship with the residents there, humans and nonhumans alike. They are regarded in different ways, but most agree on their presence. In my meager dealing with them, I feel that they are more than common spirits, but not exactly deities. Maybe they started out as spirits that decided to stick around, growing stronger as they're fueled by the emotional energy of the residents.

They can get cranky occasionally. If you notice more turmoil than usual in your area, its land spirit may need some attention. Use the spell below to create a rapport with it, possibly settling it down.

You can also appeal to them if there are community based issues that need solving. If someone goes missing, or a local thug is threatening innocent folk. In rural areas, you can ask them to bring good crops and keep the farm equipment running.

- You will need a brown or green pillar candle and your circle supplies.

- You don't have to cast a circle, but it will not only protect you, but also help raise enough energy to get the land spirit to listen.

- Hold the pillar candle and close your eyes. Think of your community's need. Think of how much better everybody's circumstances would be and how happy it would make those directly involved.

- Set the candle in the middle of your circle supplies. These are representations of the elements, so placing the candle there will concentrate its intention.

- Light the candle and make a heartfelt prayer to the land spirit.

- Spend some time meditating on your prayer and the outcome.

- When you feel like you've been heard, - a good indication of this is a feeling of peace washes over you - thank the spirit and extinguish the candle.

- Banish the circle and clean up.

Keep the candle as an offering to the land spirit every time you want to make a request. It's also a good idea to light it and say thank you when your need has been met. At least once a month, light the candle and thank it for all it's done for your area. That will keep it from throwing a tantrum.

Demonic Entities

There are several types of demonic entities, which is why I choose the word entity. The media version of demons is grossly oversimplified and dramatic. There are the spirits that ceremonial magicians summon to help them in their work, scavenger spirits, sickness demons, and disaster demons. There may be more, but those are the ones I have personally dealt with.

The demons that ceremonial magicians summon to help them in their magic are spirits that never had a body. These are the biblical demons we've heard so much about. They are their own race with their own intelligence. They do not have the same agendas or moral codes as humans so their methods may seem drastic to you. They are volatile because they are almost pure raw emotion. If you go to them for help but don't listen to what they have to say, they will get angry. If you're having a problem with one of these entities, someone probably sent it to you.

- As with the ghosts, establish dominance.

- Do a cleansing and put up a boundary.

- Once you feel it's gone, get your chosen method of divination. You need to find out who's behind the attack.

- If you know who it is, do a reversal spell from chapter six. Etch the culprit's name into the candle and imagine the entity going straight back to them.

- If you don't know who it is, do a general reversal spell and the spell to deflect psychic attack.

Unlike ghosts, these entities won't go away. They have a mission, and they intend to fulfill it. What they usually do is wait for you to drop your guard so they can get back in. Keep your protections up and reinforce them as necessary. What you are waiting for is the person behind the attack to get bored or distracted so the reversal can kick in.

Scavenger spirits are like astral parasites except they tend to accompany psychic attacks and curses to feed on the aftermath. The standard banishing should take care of them. After you get rid of them, you should find out who's behind the attack and take necessary measures.

Sickness demons have a long history. It was believed they were the sole cause of illness. Now we know about basic hygiene and infection, and it seems kind of silly. I have dealt with two of these types and found that they didn't cause the illness. They latched onto it and made it worse. Illness weakens the body's magickal defenses, making it easy for these guys to worm their way in and have a feast.

Disaster demons are born of tragedy. All that combined anger, fear, blood, and death are the perfect ingredients for a massively powerful demon. These are the scariest. They're the ones who try to manipulate things to create more tragedy so more demons can exist. When there is a disaster, even if it's far away, tune your mind into it. You will feel the entity rise out of it. Sadly I don't know if anything can be done about this except work to protect yourself and loved ones. It's way too big for one witch.

If you decide to work with any of these demons as some witches do, beware. These guys have been around a long time, and they don't think like humans. Most of them aren't out to destroy your life, but I've heard a lot of stories to that effect. Most also say that destruction was needed, they just didn't see it until later. Demons like to pick everything apart and start from scratch to create the kind of person *they* want to work with. If you decide that this is your path, tread lightly and, be careful what you wish for.

Other Entities

There are other, more specific, entities out there. If you want to deal with the spirit world, you should know everything you can about it. Sometimes they are rare or confined to a certain culture. If you'd like to dive deeper into the spirit world, the *Element Encyclopedia of Spirits* by Judika Illes is a great place to start.

Necromancy

Necromancy is a scary word, but like most in the world of magick, it's been exploited by the mainstream. It simply means to talk to the spirits of the dead. If you light a candle to a departed loved one and say a prayer for them, you're practicing necromancy. Mediums use this gift all the time to help the departed cross over into the afterlife and give their living family a bit of closure. If you decide to delve into mediumship or just want to try using a spirit board, there are steps you can take to protect yourself from invading spirits.

- Reinforce your Body of Protection.

- Always know who you're trying to contact. Inviting strangers into your space is never a good idea.

- Before you start, make it known that anything harmful will not be allowed near you. You must be assertive with angry spirits.

- When you're done, always thank the spirit and ask them to leave. If they're stubborn, do a full cleansing.

- Cleanse yourself and make sure you haven't left any portals open.

- Establish "office hours" for the spirits. Once they realize someone can communicate with them, they tend to get pushy. Task your Gargoyle Sentry to enforce these hours.

To Contact a Spirit Guardian

A spirit guardian is a spirit guide with an extra duty. If you plan to practice necromancy of any kind, asking one to join you is the smartest thing you can do.

- You will need your circle supplies and a large white pillar candle. This will be a candle dedicated to your spirit guardian so you should use it every time you practice necromancy.

- Cast the circle and pick up the candle.

- Imagine bright white light flowing into it from your writing hand.

- Fill it with love and say, "I call upon a spirit guide who will also protect me from harm as I venture into the spirit world."

- Light the candle and gaze into the flame.

- Repeat the request until you feel heard. Usually a feeling of warmth and peace will come over you, or a tingling on your face. People experience it differently, but you'll definitely feel a change.

- If you practice with a spirit board or automatic writing, you can probably get a name easily. If not, it might come to you in a dream, or just pop into your head.

Even if you can't communicate through a board or writing, make sure you talk to it regularly. Thank it for helping you and give it energy by lighting its candle. It will never let any harmful spirits near you as long as you keep a relationship with it.

Help a Departed Loved One Move On

If someone you love has just passed away and shortly after there are disturbances in your home, it's probably because they don't know what to do next. They're asking for your help because they know that you are capable.

If you can, try to contact them. Find out what their unfinished business is and see if you can help with that. If that's not possible, this spell will help them find peace and move on.

- You will need your circle supplies, something that represents your loved one, and a mirror to use as a portal.

- Set up your supplies. Place the mirror in the middle and the representation in front of it. This will draw your loved one to you.

- Invite your loved one to step in next to you.

- Cast the Banishing Circle around you both.

- Say, "Be content, your work here is done. You can go now, shining bright as the sun."

- Close your eyes. Imagine you are standing face to face with your loved one. A quiet happiness comes over you both. They begin to glow brighter and brighter as you take their hand. Lead them to the mirror and encourage them to step through. Let them know there's nothing to fear and let go of their hand. See them glow even brighter as they step through.

- Say your goodbyes and cry happy tears.

- Close the mirror portal.

- Banish the circle and clean up.

Spiritual Help

Many witches employ the aid of the benevolent spirits mentioned above. If you're on good terms with any of them, feel free to ask for their help in these situations. A prayer and quiet meditation will help you contact them. Be sure to thank them after. Gratitude is a great energy to give them. Some folks dedicate entire altars to their helper spirits, but you may not want to do that. As long as you approach them with respect and thank them after, then you will be fine.

Prayer vs. Magick

Prayer is a form of magick and magick is a form of prayer. They are related, but are not the same. Prayer is asking the spirit or god to intervene on your behalf. This is usually a crisis situation where the person feels helpless. Prayer is also used to maintain a relationship with someone's chosen gods and thank them for their help.

Magick is taking the responsibility into your own hands to manifest what you need. When you ask a god or spirit for help within a spell, they lend some of their energy to you, but you add it to the other energies you've collected and send it to its goal.

If you decide that working with spirits or gods isn't for you, that's ok. They do make dealing with harmful spirits easier, but you can do that yourself too. Just make sure you can discern which spirits are harmful and which aren't. Some spirits will choose you. They will come to you and offer to help you with your magick. Don't feel like you have to accept it if you're uncomfortable. Respectfully decline and they will go away on their own. Some will come back if you ask, but some will wash their hands of you. It's the same in the physical world. Friends come and go, a stranger helps you change a tire, or you fall in love with your worst enemy. The spirit world is no different and it helps to keep that in mind.

Takeaway

In this chapter, you've learned:

- What psychic attacks are and how to identify them.

- A spell to deflect psychic attack.

- A sachet to protect you while you sleep.

- A spell to break ties with a harmful person you've known for several lifetimes.

- A salt glow spell for protection.

- A spell using lavender bath products.

- A spell to boost your psychic powers.

- Types of harmful spirits.

- What astral parasites are and how to deal with them.

- How to deal with malevolent ghosts.

- A dead roommate spell to make friends with a ghost.

- Information on land spirits and how to appease them.

- Different types of demonic entities you may face.

- A book recommendation for dealing with spirits.

- What necromancy is and how to protect yourself if you practice.

- A spell to contact a spirit guardian.

- A spell to help a loved one move on.

- Information on seeking spiritual help.

- The difference between prayer and magick.

CHAPTER 8

Canister Spells

There might be a little dust on the bottle, but don't let it fool
ya about what's inside.
-David Lee Murphy

Canister spells are a marvelous way to pack a whole lot of power into a little container. You can use those tiny ones for portable versions or bigger canning jars. You can use bottles, boxes, and even food storage containers. The possibilities are endless.

Ingredients don't have to include herbs, though most of them do. You need things that correspond with your goal and that will fit in the canister. This can be a picture, name paper, taglock, petition, sigil, etc. The canisters can be any size or shape as long as the lid seals. Some choose canisters with metal lids because they like to burn the candle on top of it to seal the spell. How much of the ingredients to include are up to you. In the case of the herbs, a little goes a long way. Depending on the size of the canister, whatever is pleasing to you (aesthetically or energetically) is what you need. No two witches do spells the same way, even if it's the same spell.

What should you do with the canister when the spell is done? That depends on what type of work you're doing. If it's a protection canister for your home, keep it in a central location. If it's for someone else, either give it to them or store it somewhere it won't get damaged. If it's for banishing, bury it somewhere away from your house—preferably someplace you don't cross often. If it's for binding, store it somewhere dark— like the corner top of a closet—to "keep them in the dark."

Petitions

Pen and paper are your best friends when it comes to canisters. All you have to do is write down your wish, charge it, and put it in the canister with its corresponding ingredients. The petition should be short and to the point. If you need to banish something, fold it away from you as you picture the goal fleeing. If you need to draw something to you, fold it towards you as you picture the goal drawn to you.

Another type of petition is a name paper. You can use this instead of someone's picture or taglock. It should include the person's full name and birthday. If the person is on social media, you can print out their picture and use it as well.

Sigils also make great petitions. You can use the cross out

method of making one or find one that matches your intent. With the cross out method, you write the intent down. Cross out the vowels and repeat consonants. Arrange the leftover letters in a symbol that's pleasing to you. I'm not very good at this, so I usually find an established symbol to use (a pentacle for protection, dollar sign for money, heart for love, etc.).

The First Canister Spell

The traditional witch bottle has been around for centuries, with archaeological findings all over the world. It is an effective method of protection, provided your enemy is easily fooled. The idea behind it is that any curse energy or attacking spirits will see the bottle as you, attacking it instead.

- You will need a sealing canister, sharp objects like needles and pins, and your own urine. Not sanitary, is it? The point is to have so much of your own body in the canister that it acts like a decoy. A more appealing version is to take your own hair out of your brush and use that. I've done this with great results. Just make sure there's a lot of it.

- Fill the bottle, seal it tight, and bury it. Any energy sent to you will be directed to the canister and the sharp objects will act like swords to break it up.

Canister Binding

Canisters are all about containment. Do you have someone who won't leave you alone? Maybe a horrible neighbor who calls code enforcement on you every week? You can bind them and take the wind out of their sails.

- You will need a sealing canister, something that represents them—a picture, name paper, or taglock, a length of string, salt, black pepper, and poppy seeds. A black candle would be preferable, but white is universal. You don't have to cast a banishing circle, but include your supplies if you decide to do so.

- Cast the circle now if that's what you've decided.

- Set your canister ingredients before you and pick up the black candle. Say, "I charge this candle to bind (name). May (name) never bother me again!"

- Imagine black sticky energy flowing into the candle with your writing hand. When you feel you're done, set the candle aside.

- Pick up the representation and send it the black energy. Say, "You are (name). What is done to you is done to (name)."

- Place it in the bottom of the canister.

- Pick up the salt and say, "I charge this salt to block and purify any negative energy from (name)." Pour it over the representation.

- Pick up the black pepper and say, "I charge this pepper to block and destroy any negative energy from (name)." Pour it over the salt.

- Pick up the poppy seeds and say, "I charge these poppy seeds to bring confusion to (name). Every time (name) thinks of me or tries to harass me, they get distracted and forget." Pour them on top of the pepper.

- Close the canister.

- Melt the bottom of the candle a bit and fix it to the lid. Sit and focus on it for a while and say, "Within this canister, you are bound. In your mind, I can't be found."

- Light the candle and repeat this as it burns. Allow it to burn out, the wax covering the lid.

- Put the canister in a dark closet where it won't be disturbed.

Home Security Canister

- You will need a canister with a lid. This will be displayed in your home, so if you'd like to use a decorative canister or bottle, that's great. If not, a plain canister will work just fine. You'll also need plain white rice and red food coloring. A bowl and spoon for mixing these should be on hand as well. Rice is absorbent, so it's the only ingredient you'll need for this spell.

- Measure out enough rice to fill the canister and pour it into the mixing bowl.

- Mix in a drop of food dye and mix while chanting, "This home and all within it are protected."

- Repeat this, drop by drop, until you reach a nice deep red color. Make sure it doesn't get too soggy.

- Hold your writing hand over the bowl and send bright red light into it while repeating the chant.

- Continue mixing until the color looks even and dry.

- Pour it into the canister and seal it.

- Hold the canister into your hands a moment and repeat the chant a few times.

- Put in a place that everyone passes.

Since rice is absorbent, this canister pulls protective energy to you instead of radiating outward. This means it won't need recharging unless you see the rice start to go bad. If it does go bad, that means that some negativity got through. You need to dump it and start all over again.

Wet Canister to Banish Enemies

- You will need a canning jar because they seal very well, a taglock or name paper of your enemy, the hottest hot sauce you can find, and vinegar.

- Hold your taglock or name paper and send swirling black energy into it. Say, "You are (name). What happens to you, happens to (name)."

- Hold it for a few moments and charge it up as much as you can before dropping it into the jar.

- Dump the hot sauce into the canister (careful not to splash it into your eyes). Imagine your enemy catching on fire every time they try to get near you.

- If there's room in the jar, fill it the rest of the way with vinegar and seal it.

- Bury it somewhere you won't cross again. If you're from the city like me, this means gently placing it in a dumpster on a street you don't frequent.

Jinx Breaker Canister

Setting up a jinx breaker canister will help maintain good luck for your home and all who live there.

- You will need a clear canister, spring water, nails, and a white candle.

- Hold the nails and say, "I charge you to break through any curses, hexes, or jinxes." Send white light into them until you feel they're charged.

- Gently place the nails into the canister.

- Hold the water and say, "I charge you to wash away all curses, hexes, or jinxes." Send white light into it until you feel it's charged.

- Pour it into the canister and close the lid.

- Hold the candle and say, "I charge you to burn away all curses, hexes, or jinxes." Send white light into it until you feel it's charged.

- Melt the bottom of the candle a little bit and stick it to the lid.

- Light the candle and repeat, "No curses, no hexes, no jinxes," over and over until the candle has burned out.

- Leave the canister in a location that everyone in the house passes every day.

  - If the water gets murky, it means that it's absorbed negativity aimed at you. It's time to change it and recast the spell.

Canister to Repel Unsavory Spirits

Whether you have a ghost, demonic entity, or a trickster that keeps stealing your mail, this will aggressively invite them to leave and prevent them from coming back.

- You will need a canister with a lid, salt, crushed iron pills, red pepper, and black pepper. You should also have a bowl for mixing them.

- Pour enough salt into the bowl to mostly fill the canister. Add about a teaspoon each of the other ingredients.

- As you mix them, imagine the powder shooting out bright rays of both red and white energy. Say, "No spirit may enter here!" as you mix.

- Repeat until you feel it's charged.

- Pour it into the canister and seal the lid.

- Place anywhere you wish inside your home.

Protection Bottle Charm

Canister spells are fun, easy, and potent. None of these spells are difficult but each one packs a great punch. Anything can be added to them (or subtracted from them). They can be used along with another spell for a more dramatic result, and they can be miniaturized. I've seen those tiny jar and bottle spells on social media and it's a great idea, but be mindful that these are glass. A trip to the hospital is not the intended outcome!

- You will need a tiny bottle with a lid or cork (those mini ones in the jewelry section of a craft store), a charm bracelet, a red candle, salt, chili powder, a small piece of paper, and your circle supplies. These bottles usually have rings on the corks to attach to jewelry already, but if yours doesn't, you'll have to get a package of tiny screw rings and affix it yourself.

- Cast the Banishing Circle and pick up the red candle.

- Imagine red protection energy flowing into it from your writing hand. Say, "I am protected from all harm that comes for me. I am protected from now to eternity!"

- Place the candle in its holder and light it.

- Pick up the salt and chili powder, using the same chant as with the candle.

- Getting the salt and chili powder can be tricky. Crease a piece of paper and use it as a slide, pouring in a pinch at a time.

- Cork it as tight as you can and screw in a ring if it's needed.

- If you're using a taper candle, drip wax over the cork. If it's a pillar candle, dip it into the wax that pools in the center.

- Clean any remaining wax off the ring and let it cool.

- Banish the circle and clean up. The red candle can be snuffed and saved for the same spell.

- Attach it to the charm bracelet.

I have done quite a few of these and they work well, but they need to be replaced often. They tend to break or disappear when they've fulfilled their duty.

The Friendship Bottle

One of the best ways to get rid of an enemy is to convert them. We can never have too many friends, right?

- You will need a small bottle, a representation of your enemy, and pancake syrup.

- Hold the representation. Imagine it is linked directly to your enemy and say, "I name you (name). What happens to you happens to (name)."

- Put it in the bottle.

- Pour the syrup in to fill the bottle and seal it well.

- Hold it for a while and imagine your enemy being nice to

you every time you see each other.

The "I Got This" Spell

If you're feeling overwhelmed by life, negative energy is bombarding you, and you can't see an end in sight, what you need is a dose of confidence and strength. We'll use the fiery herbs of cinnamon and clove for this spell. While the peppers are great for protection and defense, cinnamon and clove are better suited for courage and personal power.

- You will need a small bottle, about the size of a whiskey shooter, a red candle, your circle supplies, salt, ground cinnamon, ground cloves, and lavender. Have a bowl and utensil on hand for mixing and either a tiny funnel or make one out of a small piece of paper.

- Cast the Banishing Circle.

- Pick up the candle. Imagine red light pouring into it from your writing hand and say, "By the powers of Mars and fire, give me the strength I need to get through this." Repeat this until you feel the candle is charged.

- Pour equal amounts of the herbs into the mixing bowl (enough to fill the bottle). Chant while mixing.

- Pour the herbs into the bottle and seal it tight.

- Drip wax from the red candle over the top and let it cool

a few moments.

- Hold the bottle over your heart and say, "I got this. I can do this. I can beat this."

- Imagine red and lavender light swirling from the bottle into your heart—red for courage and lavender for serenity.

- Banish the circle and clean up.

- Whenever you feel overwhelmed again, just hold the bottle to your heart and remember that you got this, you can do this, you can beat this.

Bottle for Grounding

Sometimes we just get frazzled. Everyday stress can take its toll, leaving us vulnerable to psychic attack, or worse. You need to send all that excess stress and anxiety into the earth to be recycled, but you can't seem to focus on doing so. This bottle will help you ease the way by pushing earth energy through your body, taking any unwanted energy with it.

- You will need a small bottle about the size of a whiskey shooter, your circle supplies, a brown candle, and some dirt in a bowl. Have a tiny funnel handy or make one out of a small piece of paper.

- Cast the Banishing Circle.

- Pick up the candle. Imagine deep brown light flowing into it from the ground (instead of your hand). Say, "Into the earth goes all my stress. I am clear and calm and totally blessed."

- Place the candle in its holder and light it.

- Pick up the bowl of dirt. Imagine the brown light from the candle flowing into it and say, "Earth to earth, the cycle round. All stress and worry, I declare ground."

- Keep chanting while you pour the dirt into the bottle.

- Seal the bottle and drip some wax over the lid.

- Hold the bottle to your heart. Imagine the brown light flowing into you, saturating your body and aura. Now imagine the light draining out through the bottom of your feet and into the ground, taking all those bad vibes with them.

- Banish the circle and clean up.

- When you're feeling extra stressed, repeat the last step.

- If you're in a state of constant stress, you may need to recharge the bottle often.

Portable Sleep Protection

Whether you're traveling or just crashing at a friend's house, this little guy will give you psychic protection and sweet dreams when you're out of your comfort zone.

- You will need one of those tiny necklace bottles, a pinch each of salt, lavender, and red pepper. Maybe two pinches, depending on the size of the bottle. Also have a bowl for mixing and a small piece of paper to crease into a funnel.

- Mix the salt, lavender, and red pepper together. Imagine white, purple, and red light twisting together and flowing into the herbs.

- Say, "Salt to purify. Lavender to calm. Pepper to protect."

- Fill the bottle and seal it well. It should be worn when you're asleep, so you may want to add some hot glue to the lid.

- Hold the bottle to your forehead and say, "Protect me wherever I sleep. Dreaming well, dreaming deep."

- Make sure it's charged and packed when you need to travel, or think you may get stuck somewhere for the night.

Takeaway

In this chapter, you've learned:

- What a canister spell is, what goes in them, and how to

dispose of them.

- How to make petitions, name papers, and sigils for your canister spells.

- The traditional witch's bottle was the first canister spell.

- A canister binding spell.

- A home security spell.

- A wet canister to banish enemies.

- A jinx breaker canister.

- A canister to repel unsavory spirits.

- A protection bottle charm.

- A friendship bottle to convert enemies.

- A bottle spell for confidence and power.

- A bottle spell for grounding.

- A spell for portable sleep protection.

CHAPTER 9

Emergency Protection

All things are ready, if the mind be so.

- William Shakespear

What is emergency protection and when do we need it? Like the Body of Protection spell, this can be done anywhere with only yourself as the tool. You've probably read in several books that you don't need tools to work your spells, while other books give detailed spells with a lot of expensive tools. They don't explain how to work magick without tools, only inform you that you can.

This is true. You can perform any spell in this book with only yourself. You are the witch, and the goodies are just fun things that lend a bit of an energy boost. You may wonder why we use the tools at all if we can just do it all in our minds. That may sound easier, but it's actually more difficult. You have to train your mind and energy to carry out the goals without any help that the tools and spells give. It takes lots of focus, but you're on the right track by working with the Body of Protection spells.

If you're sure you can't do anything without a candle or some incense, imagine yourself in your circle at home, performing the spell. Use the power you raise in the place you are now. As you gain experience, you won't need to do this anymore. When you're ready, there are a few exercises you can do to raise your own energy or borrow from other sources to perform the emergency spells.

Raising and Borrowing Energy

Raising Your Own Energy

My favorite way to raise energy before a spell is to rub my hands together until they get hot while concentrating on my goal. This can be conspicuous, so I don't recommend doing it in public.

For a more discreet exercise, sit and imagine your aura growing brighter with each breath you take. Tense up your muscles when you inhale and relax them when you exhale. When the aura is twice its normal size, you have enough energy to cast the spell.

If you're in a place you won't be disturbed (or looked at like you're crazy), drone a continuous low hum while your aura grows.

While these may take some practice, raising energy is easy once you get the hang of it. As soon as possible, you should eat and get some rest because you are using your own energy stores for this.

Borrowing Energy

So you don't tire yourself out too much, you can borrow energy from other sources. I'm not talking about vampirism, but using extra energy around you. The sun and moon are great sources. There's also extra emotional energy bouncing around the air like wi-fi. Land spirits may lend you some if you ask nicely, and you've got the whole earth underneath your feet. The possibilities are endless.

It's easiest to borrow energy from the sun during the day and the moon at night. To borrow from the sun, imagine bright golden light flowing down through the top of your head. Feel the heat all the way down to your toes. It fills you up completely until your aura is pulsating with it. Borrowing from the moon is the same, except you will feel cool silver energy fill you up until your aura pulsates with it.

Emotional energy is just thrown out there by people every day. To absorb it, imagine your aura becoming like static that only collects this extra energy and no other. It sticks to you like lint. Before your aura can absorb it, it must be cleansed so it is pure raw energy. Imagine the lint going from dull gray to bright purple, then soaking in for your use. You should practice this for a while before putting it to use. If you're not ready to filter the energy, you could take in harmful things like sickness and anger.

Borrowing from the earth is my favorite way to practice these techniques. Earth energy is stable, abundant, and always gives itself freely. Don't worry if you're indoors, or on an upper floor. Imagine pulling up from the earth toward you. Which part of the earth you're using will dictate the color of the energy—green for grass, dark brown for soil, etc. It enters through the bottom of your feet (even if you're wearing shoes) and fills you up to the top of your head. Imagine it spilling out and soaking into your aura.

These are all the tools you need to perform the emergency spells. Why use ingredients and props in the first place? Because it's easier to focus a smaller burst of energy into something that gives its own energy to the spell. This is particularly helpful for those who have trouble visualizing. Some people need something tangible that tells their subconscious that they are doing a spell and it is working. If you practice these exercises, you can do any spell you want on the go.

Cleansing Spells

The Body of Protection is your first line of defense, but it can wear down if it's bombarded with too many bad vibes. Some of them can stick to you and ruin your whole day. You'll get cranky, lethargic, and sometimes physically ill. If that happens, some emergency cleansing is in order before reinforcing your protection.

Cleansing with the Power of the Sun

- If it's daytime, take a moment to sit still. Breathe evenly and deeply.

- Imagine the golden energy of the sun flowing down through the top of your head.

- Feel the heat burning away all the bad vibes and outside influences.

- It flows down through the bottom of your feet and disappears into the earth to be quenched.

- Imagine the flow from above moving away, back into the sky where it belongs.

- Reinforce your Body of Protection.

You can cleanse a place or object with this power.

- Instead of it flowing through your body, imagine the sun's power directing itself to the arm of your writing hand and out your palm.

- Feel the heat on your hand and see the bright golden light.

- Push the energy into whatever it is that needs cleansed.

- If you still feel the heat when you're done, place your palm somewhere that can absorb it—a tree or the ground.

- Imagine the flow from above moving back into the sky.

Cleansing with the Power of the Moon

- If it's nighttime, you can use the moon for cleansing.

- Instead of hot golden light, you will bring down cool silver light.

- Imagine it flowing through like a cool shower on the inside.

- It washes away anything that's not healthy for you.

- It flows through the bottom of your feet and into the ground to be recycled.

- Imagine the moon's power moving from the ground to the sky where it belongs.

- Reinforce your Body of Protection.

You can cleanse places or objects with the sun's power. It's a gentler cleansing, but just as effective.

Cleansing with Your Own Power

Cleansing with your own power can be a little more difficult if you're low on energy. You may need to take a moment to build it.

- Sit quietly and breathe evenly and deeply.

- Imagine your aura growing brighter with every inhale.

- When you feel you have enough power stored, send it with your writing hand into what you need to cleanse.

- If you are cleansing yourself, the first two steps will do it. You're building pure energy through your entire body, not just your aura. It will automatically cleanse you.

Protection Spells

Bright red light is my favorite to use for protection, but feel free to use another if it suits you. Some use blue, purple, or black. That part is up to you. For me, red is the color of warriors.

Sword and Shield Protection Spell

This one is fun, but you may want to practice for a bit before a real emergency because you have to imagine two things at once and deal with the physical world at the same time.

- You will have to raise your own energy or borrow some, so focus on that until you feel like you have enough.

- Imagine a giant shield made of red light in front of you. It moves on its own around you to protect you whenever you need it. It will block any attacks that come at you, with or without your knowledge.

- Now imagine a giant sword made of red light next to the shield. It destroys the attacks that the shield has blocked so they can't keep trying.

Protection at a Distance

If you feel that someone you love needs protecting but they're not with you, you can give them some of your Body of Protection.

- Reinforce your Body of Protection.

- Imagine it expanding and getting stronger until you feel you can do no more.

- Imagine the excess energy sloughing off into your hand, forming a ball.

- Close your eyes and imagine the person standing face to face with you.

- Fling the ball at them. When it hits, it will explode and

surround them in their own Body of Protection.

You can also do this with objects, animals, and places.

Invisibility Magick

Anything you can imagine, you can accomplish without the use of tools, as long as you're realistic about your goals. You can't physically fly, shoot lightning bolts, or become literally invisible. Magick works in conjunction with the physical world, not against it. What you can do when you don't want to be noticed is adjust your aura and Body of Protection.

- Close your eyes and focus on both the aura and Body of Protection that covers it.

- Imagine them melding together and the light (but not the power) dimming from them.

- Now picture them becoming reflective but not glaringly so. Any negativity aimed at you will slide right past.

- This also works if someone is trying to spy on you with scrying or other divination methods.

Portable Spells

Say you're not great at working pure energy just yet, or it doesn't appeal to you. You can still use your tools and ingredients when you're not at home. The easiest way is to charge an amulet that can be activated when needed.

- You will need a piece of jewelry that you can dedicate just for protection.

- Hold it and send red light into it with your writing hand. Say, "I charge you to automatically surround me with a barrier of light when I'm threatened."

- That is its only purpose, so make sure you wear it every day. In time, you'll feel when it activates and can take extra measures if you need to.

If you have a way to carry them, you can keep tiny canisters of herbs and other tools with you. Birthday candles can be carried in a hard case to light if you need some fire energy. Matches are a good substitute as the sulfur used to make them is naturally protective. Anything can be charged and used as a tool. The power is in you, not the stuff you use.

Mind Control Barrier

There are many commanding spells on the market. The ones I despise the most are targeted love spells. All of them are an invasion of trust and privacy, but the latter is nothing short of sexual assault. All of them are about taking away your free will.

- You will need something that goes on your head like a hat, beret, hair tie, or headband. For those with piercings, eyebrow rings and earrings are ideal because they won't go anywhere.

- Hold the item and imagine the darkest black energy flowing into it with your writing hand. Say, "Only darkness fills your head when you try to penetrate mine. Alone and sinking with no lifeline." Imagine that anyone trying to control your mind gets sucked into a black hole.

If you don't have any kind of headgear available, you can work around it.

- Tap your temples and forehead while repeating the rhyme.

- Imagine the same black hole forming between the three points that your taps made.

Prayer Beads

Even if you don't follow a particular religion, prayer beads of some sort are a powerful magickal tool that you can take anywhere. They help you focus your intention amid distractions.

- All you need is a beaded necklace or bracelet. It doesn't have to be especially made for magick or other religious rites. You will put plenty of energy in when you use it.

- Repeat your intention each time you touch a bead until you come around full circle. These can be the short rhymes in this book, simple statements, or affirmations.

- There are more complicated ways to use rosaries and mala beads, but those are religion specific, and this method is best for emergencies. I use it all the time and have seen great changes, both in myself and my environment.

Eye of the Hurricane Spell

Fire is the element of protection, but it is also the element of rage. If you're sure you're being psychically attacked, cursed, or hounded by wrathful spirits, you can quickly put up this barrier around you and your space.

- Borrow energy from the element of water. Imagine a flash flood pouring in toward you. Instead of crashing down on you, it surrounds you and the area. It twists and swirls around you, gaining strength as it moves until it becomes a stationary hurricane. You are the center, and you control it.

- Any fiery rage can't penetrate this swirling wall of water. It immediately extinguishes.

- When you're out of danger, imagine it reversing until the flash flood moves backward and disappears.

Takeaway

In this chapter, you've learned:

- What emergency protection is and when you need it.

- The process of raising and borrowing energy for your spells.

- Cleansing with the power of the sun.

- Cleansing with the power of the moon.

- Cleansing with your own power.

- A sword and shield protection spell.

- Protection at a distance.

- Invisibility magick.

- Portable spells.

- A mind control barrier spell.

- How to use prayer beads to cast a spell.

- The eye of the hurricane spell to extinguish curses.

Conclusion

These spells are custom made for this book. They are meant to be experimented with and tailored to your individual needs. You may add, subtract, or change whatever you need. Even though all humans need the same basics to survive, our individual preferences make us unique. If you see red as love instead of protection, substitute it with your desired color Combine several techniques into one spell for a potent working. If you prefer to ask saints to aid you in your spells, do so. If you want to chant in Latin, go for it. Magick works with the witch. That means that it plucks your individual style from your subconscious. As you learn new things, the magick that you're experimenting with changes with you. If you try something that doesn't sit well with you, chances are that it won't work. Follow your instincts.

If you're a beginner and feel overwhelmed by all of this, that's ok. Practice the Body of Protection and Banishing Circle until you feel comfortable, then you can move on to the next spell. Work them one at a time until you feel ready to move on. Flip through the spells and pick the one you need the most to start with. Magick is not an art of instant gratification. It cannot be rushed.

Impatience is another danger. When you get impatient with your spell, things tend to go awry. Maybe you forget to close a door you've opened. Then you leave yourself open to astral parasites and bored spirits. Maybe you doubt yourself and your spell. It's not manifesting fast enough for you, so you do it again. Suddenly, everything seems to go wrong. Your spell isn't working and in fact seems to be doing the opposite of your intention. What happened? You fed your spell all that doubt and turned it sour. So please, be patient. The rewards outweigh the risks.

Because this is a book focused solely on protection spells, it may seem like practicing magick is as dangerous as the movies would have you believe. It's no more (maybe even less) dangerous than the physical world. It's just that you have to learn what the dangers are and how to avoid them. In the end, if you decide that this path isn't for you, that's okay. You won't incur the wrath of the gods and demons won't come to possess you. Every seeker must explore every path available until they find theirs.

I hope you found this spellbook informative and practical. I have tried to steer away from the massive commercialism I have seen grow as the community grows. I wanted to let you know that it's okay if you can't afford those shiny crystals and specialty oils. It's okay if having them doesn't appeal to you. You are no more or less of a witch if you found an interesting rock on the ground and decided it would be your house guardian. Witches of old didn't have all of that, and while it's great to own some beautiful tools, it's not always necessary.

Use your wit and instincts and you will be a great witch. Don't rely solely on spells for your protection. The spell is just the thing you use, but you are the creator. That means you must trust and believe in yourself. Don't suspend your own common sense just because magick is involved.

Joining the Community

So you've done magick and want to delve deeper into witchcraft. You decided that taking an active role in the community is the path for you. That's fantastic! There are many online groups you can join, and if you're more into local flavor then even rural communities tend to have one or two. If you live in a city, that's no problem.

Just remember that the witch community is just like any other. There are wonderful people to meet, but there are also some that are unstable. A few can be downright evil. Don't trust someone just because they have similar interests. If your instincts are telling you to run, do so.

A Note for Beginners

I'm sure you've noticed that this isn't a 101 book. There are plenty of those on the market and tons of information online. A beginner can do these spells, and should. The piece of advice I have for you isn't about methods, tools, or even ethics.

Where Do You Go From Here?

You may do whatever you wish, that's the beauty of spellwork. You have everything you need to protect you on your journey. If you want to use your spells to improve your situation as I have, that's great. If you want to bring justice to someone who's done you wrong, that's awesome too. Just be safe out there. Here is a bonus for when you feel like you just can't make it.

Bonus Spell for Strength

Things happen that we can't control. Life is hard, and right now the entire world is struggling. Sometimes there is nothing you can do except hunker down and weather the storm. This spell will help you gather the strength you need to get through your troubles.

- You will need a candle, (preferably red, but white is fine) pen and paper, a fireproof bowl, and a lighter.

- Pick up the candle and imagine red light flowing into it through your writing hand and say, "With the power of fire I have the strength for (name). With the power of Mars I have the strength for (name)."

- When you feel like you've put enough energy into it, set it down.

- Pick up the pen. Draw the symbol for Mars (a circle with a right diagonal arrow at the top) while chanting.

- Light the candle and set the symbol in front of it. Keep chanting while you gaze upon the symbol. When it's ready, it will flash, blur, or disappear for a split second.

- Light the paper with the candle's flame and drop it into the bowl.

- Let the candle burn out completely. Repeat as often as necessary.

My goal is to empower everyone who practices magick, no matter what path that practice takes you on. Much love and be safe.

Thank You

"Happiness springs from doing good and helping others."
— Plato

Those who help others without any expectations in return experience more fulfillment, have higher levels of success, and live longer.

I want to create the opportunity for you to do this during this reading experience. For this, I have a very simple question... If it didn't cost you money, would you help someone you've never met before, even if you never got credit for it? If so, I want to ask for a favor on behalf of someone you do not know and likely never will. They are just like you and me, or perhaps how you were a few years ago...Less experienced, filled with the desire to help the world, seeking good information but not sure where to look...this is where you can help. The only way for us at Dreamlifepress to accomplish our mission of helping people on their spiritual growth journey is to first, reach them. And most people do judge a book by its reviews. So, if you have found this book helpful, would you please take a quick moment right now to leave an honest review of the book? It will cost you nothing and less than 60 seconds. Your review will help a stranger find this book and benefit from it.

One more person finds peace and happiness…one more person may find their passion in life…one more person experience a transformation that otherwise would never have happened…To make that come true, all you have to do is to leave a review. If you're on audible, click on the three dots in the top right of your screen, rate and review. If you're reading on a e-reader or kindle, just scroll to the bottom of the book, then swipe up and it will ask for a review. If this doesn't work, you can go to the book page on amazon or wherever store you purchased this from and leave a review from that page.

PS - If you feel good about helping an unknown person, you are my kind of people. I'm excited to continue helping you in your spiritual growth journey.

PPS - A little life hack - if you introduce something valuable to someone, they naturally associate that value to you. If you think this book can benefit anyone you know, send this book their way and build goodwill. From the bottom of my heart, thank you.

Your biggest fan – **Layla**

References

Alexander, S. (2008). *The everything spells & charms book*. Adams Media.

Anderson, P. (2021). *The Jar Spells Compendium* (1st ed., Vol. 1, p. 253). Amazon Kindle.

Angelie Belard. (2020). *Hoodoo for beginners: working magic spells in rootwork and conjure with roots, herbs, candles, and oils*. Hentopan Publishing.

Angelou, M. (2008). *"I Know Why The Caged Bird Sings." Level 6*. Penguin. (Original work published 1969).

Becker, M. J. (2022). *An American Witch Bottle - Archaeology Magazine Archive*. Archive.archaeology.org.

Cabot, L., Cabot, P., & Penczak, C. (2015). *Laurie Cabot's book of shadows*. Copper Cauldron Publishing.

Cabot, L., & Thomas Dale Cowan. (1992). *Power of the witch*. Arkana.

Cohen, C. (2016, May 9). *Shots of Wit |» War and peace....* Shots of Wit.

Conway, D. J. (2001). *Wicca: the complete craft*. Crossing Press.

Dust on the Bottle. (1994). [Album]. Tony Brown.

fields. (2021, November 8). *Witches Bells: Their History, Lore and How to Use Them*. Otherworldly Oracle.

Fortune, D., & Greer, M. K. (2020). *Psychic self defense: the definitive manual for protecting yourself against paranormal attack*. Red Wheel/Weiser.

Grimes, S., & Grimes, S. (2020, March 4). *Where Did "Tibetan" Sound Bowls Really Come From?* Tricycle: The Buddhist Review.

Harris, K. (2022, August 15). *The Evil Eye*. History Daily.

Hicks, E., & Hicks, J. (2007). *The law of attraction*. Hay House.

Hunter, D. (2016). *The witch's book of power*. Llewellyn Publications.

Illes, J. (2009). *Encyclopedia of spirits : the ultimate guide to the magic of saints, angels, fairies, demons, and ghosts*. Harperone ; Enfield.

Judika Illes. (2008). *The encyclopedia of 5000 spells*. Harperone.

K, A. (2006). *True magick: a beginner's guide*. Llewellyn Publications.

Laura Tempest Zakroff. (2018). *Sigil witchery : a witch's guide to crafting magick symbols*. Llewellyn Publications.

Malbrough, R. T. (1986). *Charms, spells, and formulas for the making and use of gris-gris, herb candles, doll magick, incenses, oils, and powders-- to gain love, protection, prosperity, luck, and prophetic dreams*. Llewellyn Publications.

Mat Auryn. (2020). *Psychic Witch*. Llewellyn.

Merriam-Webster Dictionary. (2022). Merriam-Webster.com.

Morrison, D., & Blackthorn, A. (2020). *Utterly wicked: hexes, curses, and other unsavory notions*. Weiser Books.

Moskowitz, C. (2014, August 5). *Fact or Fiction?: Energy Can Neither Be Created Nor Destroyed*. Scientific American.

Penczak, C. (2004). *The witch's shield: protection magick & psychic self-defense*. Llewellyn Publications.

Penczak, C. (2006). *Instant magick: ancient wisdom, modern spellcraft*. Llewellyn.

Regan, S. (2021, December 24). *The One Thing Your Rituals Have Been Missing (& How To Make Your Own)*. Mindbodygreen.

Riva, A. (1980). *Candle burning magic: a spellbook of rituals for good and evil.* International Imports.

Swindells, R. E., & Shakespeare, W. (2010). *Henry V.* A. & C. Black.

Three Dog Night. (1973, May 11). *Shambala* [Album]. Richard Podolor.

U D, Frater. (2012). *Practical sigil magic: creating personal symbols for success.* Llewellyn Publications.

Ward, K. (2020, June 9). *Fact: You Can Totally Cleanse Your Space With Sound.* Cosmopolitan.